Battling with Nazi Demons

Werner Oder

Onwards and Upwards Publications, Berkeley House,
11 Nightingale Crescent, West Horsley, Surrey KT24 6PD

www.onwardsandupwards.org

copyright © Werner Oder 2011

Scripture quotations marked NIV are taken from the Holy Bible, NEW
INTERNATIONAL VERSION © 1978, 1984 by International Bible
Society. Used by permission of Hodder & Stoughton. All rights
reserved. Scripture quotations marked NASB are taken from the NEW
AMERICAN STANDARD BIBLE Copyright © 1960, 1963, 1963,
1968, 1971, 1972, 1973, 1975, 1979, 1995 by Lockman Foundation.
Scripture quotations marked NLT are taken from the Holy Bible, New
Living Translation, copyright © 1996. Used by permission of Tyndale
House Publishers, Inc., Wheaton, Illinois 60189. All rights reserved.
Scripture quotations marked KJV are taken from the King James
Version.

TCC chooses not to capitalise satan or related names even to the point
of grammatical incorrectness. At the same time we chose to capitalise
reference to God as 'Him' or 'His' as and when appropriate.

ISBN: 978-1-907509-21-6
Cover design: Leah-Maarit

Printed in the UK

Dedication

I dedicate this book to my wonderful wife Avril
And my beautiful children
Hanna, Markus, Anja and Anneliese.
You believed in me,
When it seemed that I had even lost faith in myself.
When I overcame,
You walked with me the road to victory.

The new generation must hear
what the old generation refused to tell them.[1]

[1] Simon Wiesenthal. The Sunflower. On the Possibilities and Limits of Forgiveness.
New York: Schocken Books, 1997. p.95-97

Content

Acknowledgments

As the son of a Nazi, I am forever indebted to two Jewish people:

One, Simon Wiesenthal, who said, *"There can be no freedom without justice and there can be no justice without truth."* [2] Through his mission I could break through the conspiracy of silence surrounding my father's crimes and find freedom through the truth.

Two, Jesus Christ, who said, *"I am the Way the Truth and the Life."* [3] Through His love I could break away from the satanic stronghold of anti-Semitism and find the way to life. I am eternally grateful to Him above all. He is the true Hero of my story, who has turned my mourning into dancing and my sorrow into joy.

My heartfelt thanks go to the many friends who have encouraged me to put my story into writing. A special thanks to my good friend David Pawson whose teaching has been fundamental in my life and who encouraged me to put pen to paper.

I am also grateful to Robin O'Neil for his thorough research of the 'School of Murder' [4] in Rabka and for his support and advice.

Last but not least, thank you to the wonderful people at *Tuckton Christian Centre* who have been behind me in this project. Your prayers and support have made this venture a success.

[2] Simon Wiesenthal, The Murderers Among Us, Pan Books Ltd, London, (1967)
[3] John 14:6 NIV
[4] Robin O'Neil, www.jewishgen.org/yizkor/Galicia2/gal018.html.

Foreword

Can any good thing come out of Nazi Austria? Well, one person did. And his story is one of the most remarkable I have ever come across.

Humanly speaking, our paths would never have crossed. Our backgrounds could hardly be more different, yet we have become blood brothers in Christ, with a friendship founded on profound mutual respect.

He could hardly have had more handicaps in life, physical, mental, emotional, social, political, racial and spiritual. But he has overcome them all, though he would be the first to say he could never have done so by himself. He is an outstanding example of what the Lord can do with a broken person when he has all the pieces.

To meet him is to meet someone who is so alive, yet has been so near death. His face and eyes sparkle. His mind is so alert, his perception so acute. He is interesting because he is interested in so much, from mechanical challenges of restoring motorbikes to an unusual appreciation of nature. He is never boring.

Though for many years he has pastored a fellowship in Christchurch, Dorset, he has a heart for the whole Church and sees only too clearly the needs of the body of Christ in Britain. This prophetic streak in his ministry needs to be heard more widely and I hope this book might open some doors for him. As the epilogue reveals, the Lord is already finding unique opportunities for him to heal the memories of European Jews, who recall with horror and bitterness the inhumanities of men like Werner's own father. For him to be humbly bringing them a vicarious apology is itself a miracle of grace.

When he asked me to write a Foreword to his autobiography I readily agreed. Indeed, I urged him to write his story in the first place, being of the limited circle privileged to know it and convinced that others would be blessed by such a unique testimony. Don't be put off by the broad canvas he paints in the early chapters; he is the child of world events. And after he has focused on his own extraordinary narrative, he will zoom out again to issues of our Western civilisation. This switching from universal to personal and back again, reminiscent of William Shakespeare's plays, is a reflection of Werner's own stage in his mind and heart.

In a word, he is a miracle of grace. What an amazing family God has. May this book introduce you to one of his most unusual sons, with whom we will share eternity.

J. David Pawson
Basingstoke
September 2008

Introduction

From the onset I knew that writing a book of this dimension would prove to be difficult. Penetrating the invisible barrier of the stony silence that characterised the Austrian post-war culture was a challenge. As an Austrian I am only too aware of the fact that old Austrians tend to have panache for conspiracy, especially when it comes to their Nazi heritage. Breaking through this conspiracy wall of silence seemed at times impossible. The graffiti on the wall of silence read,

> *We did not know anything, we did not hear anything and we did not do anything.*

There were many who did not know. But others, like my neighbours in Linz, did. Their names, like many characters in this book, have been changed. During one conversation 'Steffi' confided in me:

> *"We knew the Eichman's [5] well. They lived across the road from us on the Landstrasse. We knew many Jewish people and we knew what happened to them. We watched the Nazis torch the Synagogue during Kristall Nacht. We were afraid to say anything. Those who did were sent to Mauthausen."*

Steffi and her husband, who served in the *Wehrmacht,* are both dead now. So are my other neighbours from Linz who shared with me many things 'no one knew'. Their little contributions in my early years in Linz were instrumental in triggering off the quest for the truth, which at times seemed hidden behind an impenetrable wall. This wall was not built with human hands but stones of denial, mortared together by guilt, shame – and the mistaken loyalty to Adolf Hitler, the Austrian 'hero'. In writing this book I am reiterating the fact that '*Lying makes a problem part of the future; Truth makes it part of*

---

[5] For Adolf Eichmann see page 22

the past'. [6]

My dogged quest for the truth was more than just desiring its discovery. I hoped that by discovering the truth, I would at the same time discover my true identity - *who* I was, *why* I was born and *what* the purpose of my life was. I believed that the answer to these questions were to be found behind this wall. At first it was hard to find people who wanted to talk; there were no documents or photographs. My father, in order to cover his tracks, had destroyed all evidence. Those who had evidence either hid it, or played the *'hear no evil; see no evil'* game.

Fortunately, I soon discovered that because I was the son of a man who was respected as a hero in some circles, I could walk through the doors of these circles. Many of them were no more than the doors of hunting lodges, hidden deep in the woods of Upper Austria. There, surrounded by guns on the walls, I asked questions which soon led to discussions that seriously raised the temperature to danger level.

With my dubious political heritage I was eventually able to access classified documents hidden in vaults for over 60 years, some of them so sensitive that I was only able to examine them in the presence of the senior manager. Other secret documents were sent to me from around Europe with names recently deleted by censors monitoring my interests.

For the interest of readers, I have included photographs of these now historic documents. They are kept on file in the Jewish Documentation Centre of Yad Vashem, Israel, the Austrian Landesarchiv Linz, the Wiesenthal Centre, Vienna, and the Bundesarchiv, Ludwigsburg, Germany.

---

[6] Rick.Pitino, Basketball Coach, www.stresslesscountry.com/truth-quotes/index.html

FIGURE 1

"If we do not act, we shall surely be dragged down the long, dark, and shameful corridors of time reserved for those who possess power without compassion, might without morality, and strength without sight." [7]

---

[7] Martin Luther King Jr.

Preface

The findings of my investigation and the answer to my questions are all found in this book. Naturally, the controversial issues raised in this book will no doubt touch a nerve or two. So will the story itself, which has successfully broken through the wall of silence, bringing freedom to the people of my generation.

My decision to tell what I feel had to be told was neither to sensationalise this story nor add to the numerous books on the market that seemed to endlessly rehash the horrors of Nazi Germany. The reason for writing came from the pure and simple desire to tell the miracle God has wrought in my life, bringing good out of evil, delivering me from a prison that had confined me in its mute and dark walls. Inexplicably, amidst the confusion and personal identity problems, I discovered an uncanny inner determination to unearth the truth and, in doing so, found healing for my wounded soul and its scars that I could not explain. *'All true encounters with people leave marks in us. Some encounters leave, among other things, painful marks that are difficult to heal and leave scars.'* [8]

Today I am grateful to know that God used every encounter, despite the painful marks, to steer me toward the development of my new identity in Christ, enabling me to live with a legacy that had destroyed my father, brother and dear mother, all of whom took their secrets with them to the grave. I have learned to live with these scars that mark me out as a son of a Nazi, albeit one that has been delivered from his spiritual legacy and miraculously healed of the inevitable pain that comes with the discovery of an otherwise utterly destructive social, political and psychological heritage.

---

[8] Bormann Martin, Leben gegen Schatten, Paderborn Bonifatius GMBH, Verlag Paderborn (1996)

Chapter 1

Breaking Through the Conspiracy of Silence

The Israeli Psychologist Prof. Dr. Dan Bar-On asked the question in his book 'The Legacy of Silence, Encounters with Children of the Third Reich', *"How do the children of the perpetrators overcome the burden of their parent's guilt and live with the yoke of Silence?"* [9]

The question is valid and relevant, not just for my own life but for the life of thousands of children who are heirs of a legacy of terrorism, mass murder and genocide. My answers to these questions are found between the pages of this book, where I describe my journey from darkness to the light, and from demonic oppression to total freedom from bondage and liberty of mind.

In describing the victory over this evil heritage and triumph over the enemy of my soul, I sometimes use an aggressive tone. This, without wanting to offend, is my way of expressing deep seated convictions that have been formed over the years. At other times I avoid diplomacy in order to provide clarity of opinions which, right throughout this book, are mine.

When using language we have to be aware of the special 'Nazi Deutsch' the Germans were using, their policy was to *'never utter the words appropriate to the action'.*[10] Robin O'Neil explains this brilliantly:

> *This is the language of deception that helped shape the pattern of society... The Nazis thought up new terms and used old words contrary to their original meaning. By euphemistic presentation, they misled their enemies, victims,*

[9] 'Dan Bar-On, The Legacy of Silence, Encounters with Children of the Third Reich, Havard University Press, York, 1989, pp.231

[10] Raol Hilberg, The Destruction of the European Jews, Holmes & Meier Publishers Inc; Abridged edition edition, April 1, 1986

and those hovering on the periphery, to divert and obscure the most hideous of crimes.[11]

The first chapters of this book are given to the period of time in which my parents and grandparents lived. In doing so I have come to understand the uniqueness of our destiny. We have all been placed into history for a reason. True history, for all who care, is 'His story'. This will be explained later in the book.

Although the events described in this book are now slowly disappearing behind the horizon of history, there are nevertheless invaluable lessons to be learned. These are lessons that can be used to build, even at this stage, a better world.

To give a clear picture and provide a historic foundation to the unfolding drama, we must go back to the years before the Second World War and the rise of National Socialism in Europe where an obscure Austrian peasant became the leader of the *Nationalsozialistische Deutsche Arbeiterpartei*, (abbreviated NSDAP), generally known as the Nazi Party. As Chancellor of Germany, *Führer und Reichskanzler* from 1933 to 1945, Adolf Hitler tried to unite the German people into *das tausendjährige deutsche Reich* [12]. For a man like Hitler to become a politician of such calibre is astonishing considering his background.

---

[11] R. O'Neil, 'Rabka Four : A Warning from History, R. O'Neil, 'Rabka Four: A Warning from History (Spiderwize, UK), 2011, pp. 11

[12] See glossary.

FIGURE 2

Hitler's ancestors came fom the *Hütler* clan. The name 'Hitler' was entered in the birth register by the parish priest Josef Zahnschirm.

Hitler's obsession with the Aryan race probably stemmed from a reaction to his lowborn status. His ancestors were born in the obscure Lower Austrian village of Döllersheim. Hitler tried to keep this a closely guarded secret, always insisting *"niemand darf erfahren wer ich bin."* [13]

The reason for Hitler's paranoia about his origin

---

[13] From conversation with Eichmann's neighbours in Linz. See glossary.

possibly had its roots in the uncertainties and embarrassment of his family history. His origins have been the subject of much research, speculation and rumours. Hitler's ancestry can be traced back to his grandmother, a poor peasant woman called Anna Maria Schickelgruber, who was born in 1796 in the village of Strones, Lower Austria.

On June 7, 1837 she gave birth in Strones No. 13 to an illegitimate child who was christened the same day in the village of Döllersheim and called Alois Schickelgruber. The place for 'father' in the birth records was left empty, giving room to much speculation as to who this mysterious stranger, the grandfather of Adolf Hitler, was. Hitler's fear of discovery gave rise to the speculation that Maria's mysterious lover was her employer Frankenberger who was thought to be Jewish.

Five years later Anna Schickelgruber, Hitler's grandmother, married a wandering miller Johann Georg Hütler who was born in 1792. Hütler never legitimised the child Alois, who did not live with his parents but was brought up by the brother of his stepfather Johann Nepomuk Hütler in the small town in Spital bei Weitra.

It must have been in a cold winter when Hitler's Grandmother died at the age of 50 on January 7, 1847 in Klein-Motten. She was buried in the sleepy village of Döllersheim, the village that is said to have been the birthplace of Adolf Hitler's ancestors. Anna Maria Schickelgruber took the secret of the mysterious stranger and the real identity of her lover and grandfather of Adolf Hitler to her grave.

Her husband Georg Hütler died 10 years later in 1857. Nineteen years after his death his brother Nepomuk Hütler, who brought up Alois, appeared before the town clerk, Joseph Penker, in Weitra on June 6, 1876 with three witnesses. Hütler declared that the father of the now 39-year-old Alois Schickelgruber was his deceased brother Georg

Hütler.

Since they were illiterate, they could only pronounce the name with their heavy Austrian accent: Georg *Hütler*. The clerk duly entered in his records Georg *Hitler*, the pronunciation made *Hütler* and *Hitler* sound identical.

The following day the four men, all farmers from the area of Spital, went to the parish priest of Döllersheim, Joseph Zahnschirm, who crossed the name Schickelgruber from the Baptismal records and replaced it with *Hitler*. The priest then proceeded to fill in the hitherto empty column 'father' with Georg Hitler. All three witnesses confirmed this with 3 crosses, since they were illiterate. Immediately after that, Alois Schickelgruber adopted the name Alois Hitler, who was to become the father of Adolf Hitler.

In 1867 Alois married his first wife, a wealthy but ailing woman thirteen years his senior, at the same time carrying on an affair with a kitchen maid, Franziska. When his wife died, he married Franziska, who employed Alois' niece, a young and pretty maid called Klara Pölzl, who lived next door.

Unfortunately, Franziska developed tuberculosis and died, which gave Alois plenty of opportunity to get to know his niece more intimately. After a special petition to Rome with a plea for a papal dispensation, Klara married her uncle Alois but continued to call him 'uncle.' On April 20, 1889 Klara gave birth to a child in Braunau am Inn, a small city on the border of Germany. They called the child Adolf who was to become known throughout the world as the devil personified, Adolf Hitler.

The Hitlers lived in Vorstadt 219 Braunau until 1895 when they moved to Fischlham, near Lambach, very close to my hometown. There the young Adolf received primary education at a little country school. In 1897 the Hitlers moved to No. 16 Michaelsbergstrasse, Leonding, on the outskirts of Linz. There his parents died and were buried in the adjacent cemetery of the old parish church *Leonding* where their grave can be seen to this day.

After primary school Hitler attended the Realschule in Linz, the same school Adolf Eichmann was to attend later. Hitler following family tradition, fell in love with his niece Geli Raubal who was employed by him as a housemaid. She moved into his apartment in 1929 and later followed him to Germany as his lover. Unfortunately for her, 'Uncle Adolf' was after greater things, and the little girl from Linz had to take second place to her uncle's new flame Eva Brown. Heartbroken, Geli took Hitler's revolver and committed suicide on September 8, 1931, shooting herself through the heart.

Nevertheless, the people of Hitler's village Döllersheim loved Adolf and were proud of 'their' Führer. The little 'land', 'Döllersheimer Ländchen', was celebrated as the ancestral district of the Führer who was given the freedom of the village and honoured as its VIP, with celebrations that included one farmhouse even to be re-named: *Führerhof.*

Mark Twain's poem 'The Mysterious Stranger' could have been about the drowsy village of Döllersheim:

> *It was in 1590 - winter. Austria was far away from the world, and asleep. It drowsed in peace in the deep privacy of a hilly and woodsy solitude ... news from the world hardly ever came to disturb its dreams. We had two priests [in the sleepy village]. One of them, Father Adolf, was a very zealous and strenuous priest.... [No one] was held in more solemn and awful respect. This was because he had absolutely no fear of the Devil... Father Adolf had actually met Satan face to face more than once.*[14]

Undoubtedly applied to Hitler, Mark Twain's poem has a prophetic ring to it. Within three decades the 'Priest' of anti-Semitsm, *Führer Adolf*, who must have met with the devil face to face, led the world down the road to hell.

---

[14] Mark Twain, The Mysterious Stranger, Prometheus Books, September, 1995, pp. 42

FIGURE 3

The plaque reads:

Adolf Hitler learned to read and write here.
1895-1897.
No salvation, but death and destruction
he brought to millions of people.

Within days of Hitler invading Austria, an order was issued to the Land Registries in May 1938 to carry out a survey of Döllersheim and neighbourhood with a view to their suitability as a battle training area for the Wehrmacht. The Mayor of Allensteig and many other NS sympathisers went to see Adolf in Berlin to dissuade him from doing such a thing to his ancestral homeland where his grandmother was born, married and died. But Hitler was bent on erasing the memory of his past under the guise of building a wall against the Czechs.

In the following year the inhabitants of Döllersheim were forcibly evacuated and the birthplace of Hitler's father and the site of his grandmother's grave were rendered unrecognisable by war games that would soon plunge Europe into the darkest day of its history. Altogether 2002 people from 419 houses were forcibly evacuated. Old Austrian farmland from the villages Döllersheim, Dietreichs, Söllitz, Heinreichs, Nieder-Plöttbach mit Fürnkranzmühle, was turned into a desert. Not even the Führerhof was spared.

> *The birthplace of Hitler's father and the site of his grandmother's grave were alike rendered unrecognisable... the entire fertile and flourishing area around Döllersheim, including the little village of Strones where Anna Maria Schickelgruber was born and the cemetery she was buried in was blasted, levelled, or, to extend the Nazi-inflected metaphor of sanitation, cauterised.[15]*

Hitler did what he could to make sure that nobody would ever discover that he was the result of generational incest. He wanted to unite the German people, despite the fact that his ancestors spoke no German but the heavy dialect of the *Waldviertl.* It is a man like this who became the Führer of Germany. My family, like thousands of others, was carried along by the mass hysteria generated by this schizophrenic man who was inspired by Martin Luther's hatred of the Jews while being paranoid about the Christian church.

Because of the weakness of the German church and her ignorance over the place of Israel in the history of the world, Hitler was able to make good use of the dormant natural racism within the German people and turn them against the Jews.

With few exceptions, the Church collaborated with the

---

[15] Ron Rosenbaum, Explaining Hitler: the search for the origins of his evil, 1st edition, Random house, New York, 1998

Nazis. In neighbouring Czechoslovakia, leading Churchmen and catholic priests collaborated with the Nazis, closing their eyes and ears to the persecution of Slovak Jews in Bratislava.

Bratislava, Czechoslovakia 1940

FIGURE 4

My maternal grandparents

Pressburg

'Zuckermandl'

My maternal grandfather, Matthias Pingitzer, lived in Bratislava. Born on January 15, 1891, in a village called Nicholsdorf in lower Austria, he later moved to Pressburg, the capital of Slovakia, known today as Bratislava.

Bratislava became the seat of Hungarian Jewish

Orthodoxy under the leadership of the renowned Rabbi Moshe Schreiber. Schreiber, who served as rabbi in Bratislava from 1806 until his death and founded the influential Yeshiva of Bratislava. There, Schreiber taught that Judaism could never change or evolve. He coined the phrase '*Anything new is forbidden by the Torah.*' [16]

Although Slovakia was, like Austria, a very religious country, many of the religionists were racists. Slovakia became an independent state under the leadership of a Catholic priest, Jozef Tiso, whose one-party dictatorship was closely allied with Nazi Germany. 16 of the 63 Members of Parliament were priests.

On March 15, 1939, the Nazis invaded the Czech provinces of Bohemia and Moravia in flagrant violation of the Munich Pact.

At a conference in Salzburg on July 28, 1940, attended by Hitler, Slovak Prime Minister Vojtech Tuka and priest cum president Jozef Tiso, it was resolved to set up a National Socialist regime in Slovakia with an increased and more systematic policy of anti-Semitism.

While the catholic bishop presided over the Slovak government, trains started to deport the Jews to the death camps. Einsatzgruppe H of the Security Police and SD, under the leadership of Hermann Höfle,[17] rounded up, killed or deported the remainder of the Slovak Jews.

The aim to make Slovakia *Judenrein* was encouraged by a member of the Nazi German Foreign Office and Ambassador to the Slovak Republic, Hanns Elard Ludin.

---

[16] Hilberg, Raul. The Destruction of the European Jews, Yale University Press, New Haven, 2003

[17] As another Austrian, Hermann Höfle served in Nowy Sacz, the neighbouring village to Rabka, South of Poland. He was arrested to be tried for war crimes, but committed suicide in a Vienna prison.

Ludin[18], who arrived in Bratislava in 1941[19], convinced the Slovak government to comply with deportation of Jews for slave labor, while providing diplomatic cover for such activities.

After the hardship in the 30s, my grandfather got a job at the Nazi German embassy in Bratislava, working for the ambassador Hanns Ludin from 1941-1945. Ludin was a fanatical Nazi who belonged to the brown-shirted SA (*Sturm Abteilung*, the thuggish, violent paramilitary wing of Hitler's Nazi party, who used them as agitators to overthrow the governments of Austria and Czechoslovakia)[20]. In 1943, he was promoted to SA-*Obergruppenführer* and awarded the prestigious blood order by Adolf Hitler.

After marrying Slovak born Maria Walachovicsová, grandfather lived with his wife a humble existence in the Jewish district of *Zuckermandl* during the closing years of the Austro-Hungarian Empire. Three daughters were born to them: Maria (named after grandmother), Karoline and Helene. Though they spoke Hungarian, Slovak, Yiddish and German, they never thought of themselves as Slovaks, but *Volksdeutsche*. This title was bestowed on them by the Nazis who wanted to unite all Germans, whom they considered a superior race. Anyone who was other than German belonged to the inferior race of the *Untermenschen* (subhumans).

Like many Volksdeutsche, my grandparents were carried

---

[18] Ludin, as fully authorised Reichs minister, had been involved in the final solution and responsible for the deportation of over ten thousand Slovak Jews who were sent to their death. For the full story see Malte Ludin's documentary '2 oder 3 Dinge, die ich von ihm weiß'; absolute Medien GmbH, Oranienstr.24, 10999 Berlin, Germany.

[19] Typical for the Nazis, Ludin 'requisitioned' a large villa In Pressburg from the Jewish industrialist Stein. He lived in that villa with his family between January 1941 and April 1945.

[20] In addition to the above mentioned activities, the SA contributed to the Nazi war effort as a combat unit for the defence of the Nazi Party. They were used extensively as guards in Danzig, Posen, Silesia and the Baltic Provinces. Particular attention is drawn to their actions in the Kovno and Vilna ghettos in the guarding of Jews when digging up and burning corpses. (R. O'Neil, 'Rabka Four : A Warning from History Spiderwize, UK, 2011, pp. 194)

along by the euphoria of the unfolding Reich without foreseeing the trouble ahead. Grandfather was a weak man who admired the Nazis, especially Adolf Hitler, with whom he had an uncanny likeness. In which capacity Matthias worked for Ludin, we shall never know. What we do know is that Ludin, as the Ambassador of Nazi Germany, was responsible for the deportation of tens of thousands of Slovak Jews to the death camps. He did that with the 'blessing' of the Catholic priest President Josef Tiso.

As World War 2 came to an end, the defeat of the Nazis loomed on the horizon. When the eastern front collapsed through the advancing Russians, Tiso became jumpy and decided to flee toward the West. This forced my grandfather's employer, the Nazi ambassador H.E. Ludin, to follow suit.

My grandparents were given only 24 hours notice to get ready to flee with the Nazis. On February 5 or 6, 1945, they left everything in a great hurry and boarded the train that was to take them to 'safety'. They arrived in Linz, the capital of Upper Austria.

Linz, Austria 1938

Linz may appear to be a sleepy little industrial town on the banks of the blue Danube, but beneath its benign exterior dark forces have been hiding for decades. In the course of time they had captured certain inhabitants of Linz, turning them into the monsters which plunged Europe into the darkest period of its history. From Linz the anti-Semitic fires that soon engulfed the whole of Europe were kindled by men and women who have gone down in history as the greatest perpetrators of crimes against humanity.

Linz is the hometown of Adolf Hitler. There he went to school and spent his youth. In 1938, 38,000 people crammed into the Helden Platz (Heroes Square) greeting their Austrian hero as their Saviour with *"Heil Hitler."*

Among the crowd were my father and a local resident called Adolf Eichmann who had joined the SS on April Fool's Day, 1932. At a private political event in a pub called *Märzenkeller* near Linz, Eichmann was persuaded by Ernst Kaltenbrunner to join the Nazi Party saying: *"Du gehörst zu uns"* (you belong to us). Kaltenbrunner, as the head of the Austrian SS and later chief of the SD,[21] became responsible for the murder of thousands of people at Mauthausen. Eichmann became infamous as the number one among Nazi officers whose sole task was to deal with the 'Jewish Question'.[22]

In Linz, Hitler commissioned the building of the concentration 'mother camp' at Mauthausen across the Danube of his hometown of Linz.

When my grandparents disembarked from the train in Linz, they were assigned a small flat in the SS block at *St.Georgen an der Gusen,* next to the biggest and most brutal Nazi concentration camp complex on Austrian territory. In the three giant labour camps Gusen I, II, III more than 37,000 people died, providing forced labour for Hitler's insane war machine. Did they know that they had arrived at the centre of human extermination in Austria: Mauthausen? We will never know.

---

[21] The (SD) Sicherheits Dienst was a criminal organisation which killed any enemies of the Reich. For Kaltenbrunner see pp. 24, footnote 20

[22] Eichmann, who was responsible for the transportation of 6 million Jews to the death camps, fled to Central America. Along with hundreds of other war criminals, he enjoyed the protection of the Argentine government. He was captured in Argentina in 1960 and tried in Israel, where he was hanged for his crimes a few minutes after midnight on June 2, 1962

FIGURE 5

Rescue those being led away to death; hold back those staggering towards slaughter. If you say, "But we knew nothing about this," does not he who weighs the heart perceive it? Does not he who guards your life know it? Will he not repay each person according to what he has done? [23]

---

[23] Proverbs 24:11 NIV

Mauthausen[24] was mostly used for extermination through labour of the *intelligentsia,* who were educated people and members of the higher social classes in countries subjugated by the Nazi regime during World War II. In mid-April 1945, when the whole Mauthausen[25] complex was in total chaos due to the mass evacuation from other concentration camps, cases of cannibalism were reported. These were the conditions in and around the new home of my grandparents who crammed into their small flat provided by the SS. Their 'employers', however, Slovak president Tiso and Nazi Ambassador Ludin, travelled a few miles south to the market town of Kremsmünster.

To accommodate their 'heroes' from the east, the Nazis 'requisitioned' properties for them. For the Czech president they provided sumptuous accommodation in the large monastery *Stift* Kremsmünster. There, Tiso rested from the exhausting task of fleeing from the Russians who had invaded Pressburg and were threatening Vienna. Though his forty strong Slovak guard kept him safe for the time being, he never felt safe. Confiding in one of the Catholic priests, he spoke of his amicable relationship with Hitler, who encouraged him to do his best for his people. (This usually meant, in true Nazi fashion, to do the worst for the Jewish people). On April 16, 1945, Tiso learned that the fast approaching Allied Forces were considering him and his ministers as war criminals in relation to the events in Poland. His only resolve was to flee further to the West, in the hope of falling into the hands of the British or American forces.

---

[24] To this day it is not clear how many people died in Mauthausen, which was a category three camp, with Rückkehr unerwünscht policy. Estimates range between 100000 to almost two million who were murdered by the Nazis.

[25] Mauthausen prisoner Hans Marsalek testified in his affidavit that the dying camp commander Franz Ziereis confessed on his death bed on May 23, 1945: 'According to an order by Himmler, I was to liquidate all prisoners on behalf of SS Obergruppenführer Dr. Kaltenbrunner.' (Kaltenbrunner was convicted and hanged in Nürnberg for crimes against humanity on Oct 16, 1945, http://www.nizkor.org/, p.792)

While Tiso was fretfully wringing his religious hands in *'The Stift'*, Ludin tried to hole up in *Schloss Kremsegg*. The *Schloss* belonged to an exiled Countess who left the estate in the hands of her manager who was forced to surrender the property to the Nazis. When it became clear that the war was lost and that the Americans were approaching, Ludin tried to turn the Schloss, with the help of the manager, into a hiding place. A special room was set aside, with concealed doors. There he hid until the worst was over.

FIGURE 6

At the same time the American 41st Recon Squad of the 11th Division US Army liberated Mauthausen on May 5, 1945. They rounded up the inhabitants of the SS estate and force-marched the people to the nearby concentration camp. There they made my grandparents, among others, watch former SS officers dig graves for the victims of their brutality while death camp survivors were milling about after getting their revenge on many Nazi officers.

One of the liberated survivors of Mauthausen was Stefan Kuster, prisoner No. 131307. He was arrested by the Nazis for belonging to 'the Quiet People's Resistance' in Poland. This organisation engaged, as the name suggests in quietly resisting the Nazis, refusing to swear allegiance to the German Reich and for speaking against the existence and atrocities of the death camps. He was sent to Mauthausen where he was tortured, but managed to survive.

The Most Hated Jew in Linz, Simon Wiesenthal

FIGURE 7

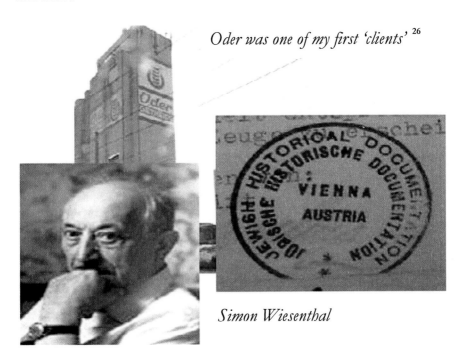

Oder was one of my first 'clients' [26]

Simon Wiesenthal

Another survivor of Mauthausen was his fellow prisoner, the Galician Jew *Simon Wiesenthal*. After surviving the death camp, Wiesenthal settled in Linz. While trying to

[26] Wiesenthal S, The Murderers Among Us, Pan Books, London 1969, pp. 271

recover from his ordeal, he opened the *Dokumentations Zentrum* in the *Landstrasse*. From there he gathered evidence against war criminals who were responsible for the Holocaust and carnage in Europe. He became known as the *Nazi Hunter.*

Wiesenthal was often asked to explain his motives for becoming a Nazi hunter. He explained his reason in the home of a former Mauthausen inmate, who later became a well-to-do jewellery manufacturer.

After dinner his host said, "Simon, if you had gone back to building houses, you'd be a millionaire. Why didn't you?"

"You're a religious man," replied Wiesenthal. "You believe in God and life after death. I also believe. When we come to the other world and meet the millions of Jews who died in the camps and they ask us, 'What have you done?' there will be many answers. You will say, 'I became a jeweller,' another will say, 'I have smuggled coffee and American cigarettes,' another will say, 'I built houses,' But I will say, '*I did not forget you.*'" [27]

According to his book, *The Murderers among us,* one of the first targets of Wiesenthal's pursuit were members of my own family. The person he was looking for was SS-*Untersturmführer* Herman Oder, SS- number 86,051. At this stage Wiesenthal did not know that Herman was my father's older brother who joined the SS in 1938 but was no war criminal. In fact Hermann was married to a Jewish woman. He adopted her child and gave both of them his name, thereby saving them from the Holocaust.

Because Hermann was a well-known businessman in Linz, Wiesenthal, who mistook him for Wilhelm, had Hermann arrested. At his arrest he was living in his wife's Jewish Villa in Linz.[28] Even though Hermann spent some

---

[27] Interview with Clyde Farnsworth, New York Times Magazine February 2, 1964
[28] Simon Wiesenthal, Doch die Mörder leben, Herausgeber Josef Wechsberg, Droemerschen Verlagsanstalt TH. Buch-Nr.5848/11, pp. 305

time in *Untersuchungshaft*, the mistake was soon discovered and he was released. The hunt for his brother Wilhelm continued.

Living in Linz within very close proximity of Adolf Eichmann's former flat in Bishofstrasse, Wiesenthal embarked upon his assignment which made him the most unpopular survivor in Linz, if not in the whole of Austria. One former member of the German Wehrmacht told this author repeatedly, "*Der Wiesenthal war in Linz nicht beliebt.*" Wiesenthal was not very popular in Linz, which was probably due to Wiesenthal's motto:

> *There can be no freedom without justice and there can be no justice without truth.' he said. "When history looks back, I want people to know the Nazis were not able to kill millions of people and get away with it.*[29]

With Wiesenthal gathering evidence, the Americans started to look for the perpetrators of the Holocaust. Arriving in the town of Kremsmünster, they arrested three wanted men, among them Hanns Elard Ludin and Josef Tiso. The third man, who was on Wiesenthal's priority list of wanted men, later became a major player in my life. Unfortunately for Tiso and his henchmen, the Americans extradited them together with Hermann Höfle, another criminal on the loose, to Czechoslovakia in 1946. There they were sentenced to death in 1947.[30]

Seeing that his boss was facing the rope, grandfather, for all his weaknesses, showed amazing dexterity by swiftly occupying Ludin's chambers in Schloss Kremsegg. For a brief moment the Schloss was theirs. A dream had come true. However, their joy of luxury was short lived due to the return

---

[29] Simon Wiesenthal centre, About Simon Wiesenthal, www.wiesenthal.com
[30] Ludin was hanged for the deportation and death of over 60 000 Slovak Jews on December 9, 1947. Tiso also was found guilty of treason and crimes against humanity. He was hanged in his clerical costume on April 18, 1947. Höfle too committed suicide before his trial.

of the owner, Countess Kinsky, who arrived from exile to take possession of her Schloss once again. She graciously agreed to let grandfather occupy some humble rooms in the *Gesindehouse*, the servants' quarters. There they tried to rebuild their lives, waiting for their three girls to come home from the war.

Maria, the eldest, was the first to arrive back. She was a very kind woman who was duly employed by the Countess as a chambermaid.

When Helene arrived, her parents discovered that she was pregnant. The father of the child was 'Stefan', the Polish survivor of Mauthausen. Damaged by his experience in the death camp, Stefan broke all his promises of marriage and disappeared to America, never to be seen again, leaving Helene to carry the shame and fend for herself and her illegitimate child. In 1946, Helene gave birth to a delightful baby girl, my cousin Ricki.[31] Ricki's delightful nature was like a ray of joy amidst the gloom of the post-war environment my family lived in. Her laughter filled the air and her positive nature made her a delightful companion, though she was never told that her father was a hero.[32]

Karoline also returned from the war. It became apparent that she too was badly damaged by experiences she hardly spoke about. When she did, her memory was sketchy. Somewhat incoherently, she would speak about her flight from Berlin... *being shot at... dressing up as an old woman ... running from Russian rapists.... climbing over dud bombs... walking at night... hiding during the day...and a lover who did not return from the war...* She never divulged to anyone where she had been, what she

---

[31] Though we share an uncommon heritage - Ricki the daughter of a Nazi victim and I, the son of a Nazi criminal, we both share a faith in the Jewish Messiah and love for His people.

[32] Helene however was never able to see the wonderful gift of a little girl who was a ray of sunshine in her dark world. All she saw was shame, all she felt was pain. She is still alive today, a lonely woman who was unable to come to terms with her past. She is another victim of the Nazi past which took its toll on our family, destroying all those who were unable to put the past to rest.

had done or what happened to her. Arriving in Kremsmünster, she was glad to be reunited with her parents in such an idyllic environment where everyone played the pretend game of being aristocracy. For a short period of time the family's delusions of grandeur provided some distraction from the surrounding horror and poverty.

Despite our poverty and shame, the Schloss was an island of bliss amid the migration of broken and homeless people - survivors of Russian prison camps arrived in rags, looking for relatives. Holocaust survivors were looking for revenge, war criminals tried to hide, while scores of refugees scrambled to find a place to live. Amidst all this the Allied Forces tried to establish a police force that was to keep law and order while at the same time trying to arrest fleeing Nazi fugitives on their way to South America.

While Karoline tried to recover from the horrors of her war experience, she met a 'local musician', a charming man. His musical ability on the zither appealed to her torn emotions, his promises made her forget her shattered dreams. Little did she know that he was a killer on the run, a wanted man on Wiesenthal's priority list. Throwing caution to the wind, she gave herself to a man she hardly knew. When the police came for him, her love for him blinded her to the reality that he was a murderer. He was the 'third man' to be arrested in the small town of Kremsmünster.

The Third Man

FIGURE 8

¦ *Rev. Josef Tiso* *Hanns E. Ludin* ?

On June 28, 1914 the Austrian successor to the throne Franz Ferdinand was gunned down by a Serb terrorist in Sarajevo. This triggered off the First World War which has been prophesied as the 'beginning of the end.' Though it was not the end of the world, it certainly was the end of the Austro-Hungarian Empire.

With the collapse of the Austro-Hungarian Empire, Austria became a republic that was governed by Engelbert Dollfuss who led the nationalistic totalitarian movement of Austria. He was opposed to the fascist movement of Adolf

Hitler in neighbouring Germany and declared the Nazi party illegal in Austria.

Hitler, the Austrian chancellor of Germany, was anxious to annex his home country to Nazi Germany as soon as possible. Unfortunately for him, the Austrian Government under Dollfuss' leadership was strongly opposed to Nazi politics. Hitler's response was to deploy Nazi agitators to destabilise Austria. Since these Nazi sympathisers were engaged in illegal activities against the state of Austria, they were called *die Illegalen* (The Illegals), a term used for thugs who became the heroes of Nazi Austria. As SS underground units, commanded by Ernst Kaltenbrunner, they would attack government buildings or police stations and then blame this on what they called Bolshevik Jews. The Austrian Police, who knew it was the Nazis and not the Jews, would then arrest *die Illegalen* and throw them into jail. For Hitler this was the best publicity. It made his supporters look like martyrs at the hands of the 'evil Jews.'

One of those 'illegal' Nazis was a certain Wilhelm Oder who had joined the NSDAP in 1928 as member No. 6,271,713, two years after he married the beautiful Lilly Kump. They had two children, Wilhelm and Peter, whom Lilly tried to keep alive during the years of depression. She did this without the help of her husband who was too committed to carrying out the secret terrorist policies of the NSDAP.

However Dolfuss stood firm against the Nazis and issued a death sentence upon all Nazi agitators. This was a thorn in Hitler's evil eye. Just one year after Hitler came to power in Germany, he gave the order for the assassination of Engelbert Dollfuss. On July 24, 1934, the Nazis assassinated the Austrian Chancellor.

FIGURE 9

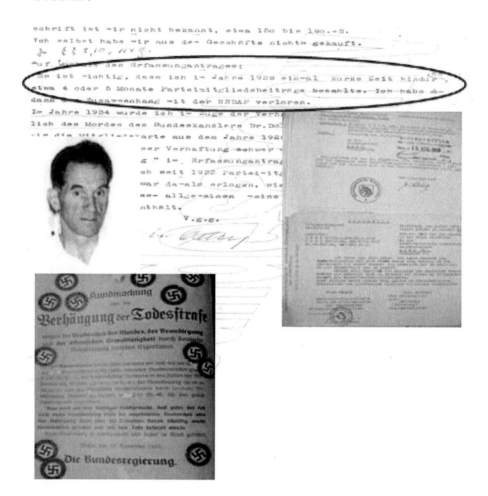

With Dolfuss dying, the rest of the cabinet ministers managed to escape and raise the alarm at the Ministry of Defence, who surrounded the building, arresting Nazi agitators and other sympathisers who were behind the assassination of the Austrian chancellor. Among those arrested was Wilhelm Oder who was charged with treason against the newly founded Republic of Austria.[33] He was

---

[33] Bundesarchiv Ludwigsburg, War trial documents 6AR-Z34/61 pp. 54

condemned to death and faced the firing squad.

After the assassination of the Austrian chancellor, Austria was in a precarious position. National Socialism, though still outlawed in Austria, was on the rise, promoted by Hitler from neighbouring Germany. The new Austrian chancellor, who replaced his assassinated predecessor, was the Tyrolean Karl von Schuschnigg, who tried in vain to keep the Nazis at bay. Hoping to buy time for Austria, Schuschnigg made a treaty with Hitler agreeing the release of all Nazi prisoners. This agreement sealed the fate of Austria who released 17,000 Nazi-political prisoners, among them my father. Delighted, the Nazis prepared a welcoming party for Adolf Hitler in the form of the *Anschluss*. It was no invasion; it was a homecoming street party for Adolf who annexed Austria on March 12, 1938. Touched by their loyalty, Hitler rewarded the hitherto illegal party members with the honour of the blood order. [34]

City of the Damned

From then on Linz became the launching pad from where evil men, for all their religiosity, plotted the death of the Jews and where they built the infamous death camp Mauthausen. Mauthausen was to become the central camp which the Austrian SS referred to as the mother camp, serving 49 other concentration camps in Austria. Adjacent to Mauthausen were 3 forced labour camps of *Gusen I,II,III* in which thousands were worked to death. [35]

[34] Among those honoured was Hermann, who was awarded the Bloodorder in recognition of his loyalty and services to the Reich. He went on to become a leading light of the ODESSA in 1948.

[35] Although the horrors of Mauthausen were surpassed by Auschwitz, the tragedy of the Holocaust cannot be computed by the sheer numbers of people killed.

FIGURE 10: CITY OF THE DAMNED

Anschluss Linz

March 1938

Very few people were true Nazis, but many enjoyed the return of German pride, and many more were too busy to care. I was one of those who just thought the Nazis were a bunch of fools. So the majority just sat back and let it happen.[36]

---

[36] Dr. Emanuel Tanay, A German's Point of View on Islam,
www.godlikeproductions.com/forum1/message521882/pg1)

On his birthday of the same year, March 18, 1938, which he shared with Adolf Eichmann, Wilhelm Oder joined the SS STURM 55/5 in the small town of St. Pölten. No longer an underground SS soldier, he was among the Nazi agitators who began to attack Jewish properties on the night of November 9, 1938, in what became known as the infamous *Crystal night*.

The night of the broken glass signalled the start of International anti-Semitism which was to result in the murder of 6 million Jews and Christians.

On July 1, 1940 he joined the 8th Totenkopf Standarte, the division which was formed in 1939, and put in charge of death camps such as Dachau and Mauthausen. He was sent to Dachau for training. As a member of the Totenkopf Einsatzgruppe he wore the death head symbol on his collar and his ring. These symbols stated '*We carry the death head as a warning to our enemies.*' [37] As part of the Death Head Division's assignment he left for Dachau in November 1940.

On June 1, 1942, he abandoned his beautiful wife and two children and resigned his membership of the Church.[38] He effectively turned his back on God. In doing so, he sold his soul to the devil who began to use him to make life hell for the innocent victims of the Jewish community through the death squads of German anti-Semitism.

---

[37] See Figure 11
[38] Erich Ludendorff, early companion of Hitler called this 'Erlösung von Jesus Christus' (deliverance from Jesus Christ)

FIGURE 11

SS- Rottenführer
Wilhelm O d e r ,
Schule der Sicherheits-
polizei in
Rabka- Bad, GG.

Rabka, den 1. Juni 1942

An das
Amtsgericht "Kirchenaustrittsstelle"
St. P ö l t e n , ND.Ostmark.

          Ich erkläre mit heutigen Tage d.1. Juni 1942
meinen Austritt aus der Kirche.
          Die bezügliche Austrittsbestätigung erbitte ich
postwendend an meine obenangeführte Adresse bei gleichzeitiger Be-
kanntgabe event. erwachsender Spesen die ich gesetzten Falles sofort
anweisen werde.
          Zur Durchführung meiner Erklärung gebe ich nach-
stehend meine Geb.Daten bekannt.

Einschreiben

Heil Hitler

Oder

SS- Rottenführer

Wilhelm Oder, geboren am 18.3.1905
r.kath. Vöcklabruck,verh.Familien-
wohnsitz(ordentlicher)St. Pölten,
Mühlweg 9,ND.Ostmark.

*SS motto: "We carry the death's head on our black cap as a
warning to our enemies and an indication to our Führer that
we will sacrifice our lives for his idea.*[39]

[39] Alois Rosenwink, de.wikipedia.org/wiki/Alois_Rosenwink

Chapter 2

FIGURE 12

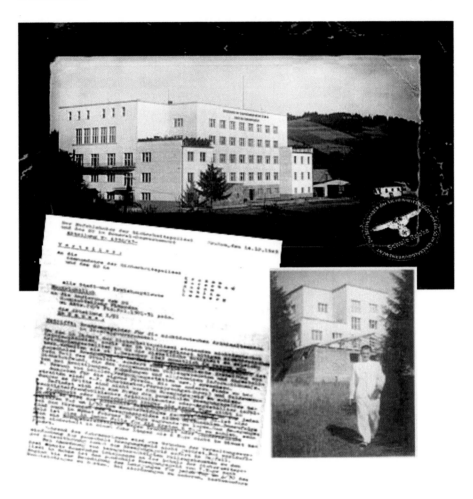

Man cannot take too much truth at the time, especially truth about himself. Our capacity for self deception is gigantic. [40]

Rabka, Poland 1941

From Dachau, Wilhelm Oder was posted as *Unterscharführer* of the German SS to the small town Rabka,

---

[40] T.S.Elliot

Poland. In 1941, Bad Rabka was a small health resort located on both sides of the Raba River, halfway between Krakow and Zakopane. At the outbreak of war there were approximately 7,000 inhabitants in the town. In the 1930's, Rabka had a Jewish population of 120 families (about 500 souls) who met at the synagogue. In 1929, the Tarbut Hebrew School was founded and it soon became the centre for the Jewish young people.

During the first months after the occupation of Poland, the Commander-in-Chief of the German Security Police, SS-Brigadier-Führer Bruno Steckelbach, founded the Sipo-SD School (*Sicherheitspolizei-Sicherheits Dienst*)[41]. The SD was close to the Slovak border in Zakopane, a winter resort at the foot of the high Tatra, which had a Jewish population of about 1,500. Relatives and friends of the local Jews had moved from the larger towns to areas less exposed to persecution elsewhere. This was an age-old custom of the Jews, who sought protection and comfort in numbers in times of stress.

The purpose of the school was to train selected candidates of Sipo-SD, collaborating Ukrainians (such as the *Volksdeutsche* brothers Johann and Wilhelm Mauer), Police Officers and other Sipo-SD personnel, who were instructed by the head of the SD SS *Obergruppenführer* Reinhard Heydrich on July 2, 1941:

> ...*the immediate goal of the security police is the pacification of all newly occupied areas ... to be executed are all professional politicians and ... Jews...*[42]

Among the 'students' were intelligence-gathering

---

[41]Translated: Command of the Security police and Security Service in the General Government, School of the Security service. This 'school' incorporated three of the most feared organisations: the SiPo (Security police), the Gestapo (secret state police) and the SD, (Security Service). All three organisations were infamous for unwarranted arrests and murder of enemies of the Reich, i.e. Jews, Christians and civilians who did not tow the party line. My father belonged to all three.

[42] Gordon Williamson, The SS, Hitler's Instrument of Terror, Sidgwick & Jackson, 1995, pp. 226

sympathisers ('V'-Agents) under the leadership of the Commandant, SS *Hauptsturmführer* Hans Krüger. These V agents were Nazi spies who would lurk about the town and report any Jew they spotted.

One of the Nazi units in Southern Poland was the 13th *Gebirgsjäger* (mountaintroops), made up of Germans and Austrians who were familiar with mountainous terrain. These troops raised many sympathisers among the Polish mountain people, the Gorals[43], whose minds they poisoned with anti Semitism.

The SD School later moved to Rabka where it 'requisitioned' [44] the Jewish religious institution for children, the Tarbut Hebrew School, which was situated near the Chabowka railway station. In the late autumn the school moved to new and much larger premises in the 'Theresianeum' (also called 'Thereska'), a high school for girls. The four-story building was located in the northern part of the town called Slonna, on a tree-covered slope alongside the Slonna River, which flowed into the Raba River.

Within days of the Rabka School becoming operational, a large black flag with a swastika was prominently mounted on the roof. In large black letters, the following was displayed across the top floor of the building:

BEFEHLSHABER der SICHERHEITSPOLIZEI und des SD im GG SCHULE der SICHERHEITSPOLIZEI.[45]

The Rabka School, since its establishment in Zakopane, had introduced specialised Ukrainian and Austrian instructors, namely, the Mauer brothers and my father, who

---

[43] After the defeat of Nazi Germany it was these Nazi sympathisers who continued the persecution of the Jews in post-war Poland

[44] 'Requisitioned' was the political correct term for confiscation, theft, and commandeering of properties belonging to civilians.

[45] See glossary

joined the school in March 1942 as SS *Unterscharführer.*[46] He and SS Hauptscharführers Walter Proch acted as deputies to the school commander, a man with a Jewish name, Wilhelm Rosenbaum. He was married to a woman from Rabka, Anne Marie Bachus. The strange thing is that the man appointed to be the janitor of the school had a Jewish name and Jewish features. Wilhelm Rosenbaum was always teased by his deputies about his Jewish name. If he was a Jew, then the saying is true that the Jews have always been their own worst enemies.

The female contracted staff (and later witnesses) were mostly young Jewish women, except Käthe Engelmann, secretary to Rosenbaum, who was German. The Jewesses Sarah Lucia Goldfinger and Ada Rawicz (nee Ada Peller) were employed as cleaners. Sarah Goldfinger also worked as a maid and nanny in the household of the SS *Hauptscharführer* Proch. Lisa Kaufman, who worked as secretary in the school, was the sister of Wilhelm and Johann Mauer who were members of the *Einsatzgruppen.*

Wilhelm Oder, a good musician, soon attracted the attention of Rosenbaum's secretary Käthe Engelmann. Though he was still married to Lilly, whose boys were forced to join the training camps of the Hitler youth, Käthe became pregnant. Not wanting the child to be born on Polish soil, Wilhelm sent Käthe to Germany where she gave birth in Hamburg to my half sister Gesa on May 22, 1943.

Behind the façade of a 'school', the Theresianeum was to become the training area of the *Einsatzgruppen,* where German, Polish, Ukrainian and Austrian soldiers were taught execution techniques. The two *Einsatzgruppen* members

---

[46] Some people say that these ranks Unterscharführer (Corporal) Oberscharführer (sergeant, staff sergeant) were fictional, 'in reality they were high ranking officers'. The fact is that the SS maintained and used these low ranks to do their dirty work. These low ranks were chosen to bear the brunt of any prosecution, thus buying high ranking officers time to escape to Argentina and Chile. There they lived the lives of millionaires, while the low ranks were either imprisoned or executed.

Johann and Wilhelm Mauer were experienced sadists. After participating in machine gunning 12,000 people in what became known as the 'Blood Sunday' of Stanislaw, they forced the remnant of the Jewish community to pay 2,000 Zloty for spent ammunition.

The training courses were run by my father who was known as the *Genickschuss Experte*[47] (shot in the neck expert). He and his team blindly followed Himmler's dictum: '*The Jews are the eternal enemies of the German people and must be executed.*' [48]

In 1966, Wilhelm Rosenbaum confirmed at his war crime trial in Hamburg the existence of special courses for the Waffen-SS:

Unterscharführer Wilhelm Oder was in charge of this course. Although Oder was on Rosenbaum's staff, he was directly answerable to Dr Schöngarth (BdS) Krakow. He was at the Rabka School from autumn 1941 until March 1943 (when Rosenbaum was removed). Oder did much of the killing as an example to his student conscripts. Oder was an expert in the 'shot in the neck' technique. He would show his students how to do this using his pistol, a Walther PPK calibre 7.65, shooting Jews at a distance of 10-20 centimetres. Also used were various assortments of machine pistols.[49]

---

[47]The man, who taught my father his 'work' of shooting defenceless victims in the neck, was probably the Austrian SS.Unterscharführer Maximilian Grabner. In 1946 Grabner was extradited to Poland and hanged for developing this technique of murder in Katowice (50 km from Rabka) and Auschwitz. Grabner's excuse would have been laughable would it not be for the thousands he murdered: 'Ich habe nur mit Rücksicht auf meine Familie mitgewirkt an der Ermordung von 3 Millionen Menschen. Ich war niemals Antisemit.' (I have only taken part in the murder of 3 million people in the interest of my family. I never was an Anti-Semite. de.wikipedia.org/wiki/Maximilian_Grabner)

[48] Gordon Williamson, The SS, Hitler's Instrument of Terror, Sidgwick & Jackson, 1995, pp. 232

[49] Robin O'Neil, www.jewishgen.org/yizkor/Galicia2/gal018.html. (Although Rosenbaum testifies to Wilhelm Oder using a Walther PPK, 7.64, it is more likely that the weapon used was the Luger P08 Parabellum, cal 7.64 which was favoured by the SS.)

FIGURE 13

All forms of murder were used: shootings, hanging and beatings. In the continuous roundups from neighbouring villages, victims were rounded up and brought to the school to be executed in the school grounds.

Some Hasidic Jews, when rounded up by the SS, would put on their Sabbath clothes, dressing as they would for a special occasion. Led by their Rebbe, they would walk stoically behind their leader who carried the ancient Scrolls of the Torah while mothers carried their little children. They walked in dignity, facing what was to come with the courage of those who believed in a better world. Arriving at the school they were received with particular cruelty and made to run the gauntlet of the SS and Ukrainians who beat them mercilessly on their path to the pits that had been dug in the woods. With their scrolls cut into shreds, they were shot and fell into the pit crying, *"Shema Yisrael."* [50]

The SD school of Rabka has since been appropriately termed as the Rabka School of Murder.[51]

FIGURE 14

The Lord, the God of our ancestors was angry with Judah and let you defeat them. But you have gone too far, killing them without mercy, and all Heaven is disturbed [52]

---

[50] The first two words of the Torah: Hear O Israel, the Lord our God, the Lord is One. (Dr. R. O'Neil, Rabka Four: A Warning from History, Spiderwize, UK, 2011, pp. 79)

[51] Ibid, pp. 37: 'From special training camps, such as the SD school in Zakopane/Rabka, came some of the most brutal criminals in history. We must remind ourselves, contrary to popular belief, that it was the Sipo-SD and not the Allgemeine-Schutzstaffeln (General SS) that were responsible for Jewish murder'.

[52] 2.Chronicles 28:9 (NLT)

Rabka School of Murder[53]

At first the Germans murdered the Jews openly as part of a national brutalisation of non-Aryan races. This was however changed when General-Lieutenant Heinrich Kittel commander of the 462 *Volksgrenadier Division* gave orders forbidding such executions from taking place in the open where people could look on. He said, *"shoot people in the woods or somewhere where no one can see."* [54]

From then on the trainees of the Police school practiced executions in a clearing in the woods. SS students shot Jews and Poles rounded up by the Gestapo, while SS *Untersturmführer* Rosenbaum observed students' reactions with clinical detachment. If a student flinched, he was removed from the execution squad and sent to the front. The SS men were being hardened at Rabka so they would become insensitive to blood and the agonizing cries of women and children.

An example of this was another Austrian-Viennese Police Secretary Walter Mattner who participated in the mass murder of 2,273 Jews in Mogilew, October 1941. Afterwards he wrote to his wife:

At the first wagon load (of Jews) my hand was shaking. But after the tenth wagon I aimed and calmly shot at the many women, children and infants. [55]

The job must be done with a minimum of fuss and maximum of efficiency; that was a *Führerbefehl* - the Führer's order. Many soldiers suffered nervous breakdowns as a result of seeing the suffering they inflicted. Others broke down in tears when they heard the children pleading, *"Mummy, mummy, help me."* Some, without conscience, pressed the

---

[53] For a detailed account of the School of Murder see Dr.Robin O'Neil's book The Rabka Four. A Warning from History, Spiderwize, UK, 2011

[54] Jpost.com, Tuesday Jul 24, 2007

[55] Walter Mattner SS & Polizeiführer, Mogilew, Ukraine, www.spiegel.de/international/germany/0,1518,542245,00.html

trigger with a cynical grin.

Early summer in 1942, SS Rosenbaum ordered all Rabka's Jews to appear at the local school to 'register.' The sick and the elderly would be 'deported' or shot; the others would labour for the *Wehrmacht*. Toward the end of the registration, Rosenbaum appeared accompanied by two deputies, Wilhelm Oder and Walter Proch, to 'process' the Jews.

FIGURE 15

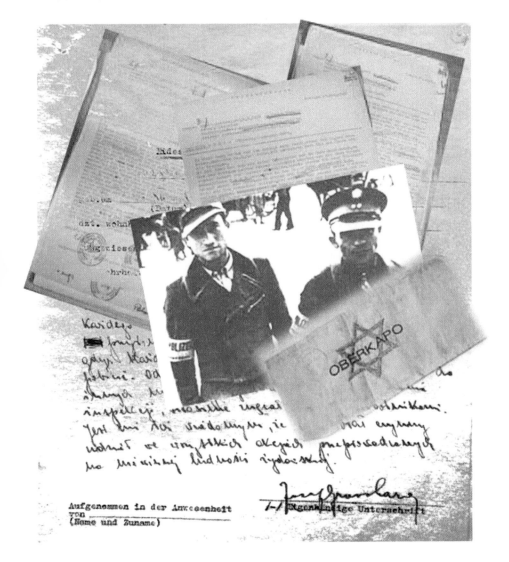

One of the most tragic stories I came across during my investigation is that of a Jewish family in Rabka, who shared the same name as the SS school Janitor cum commander: Rosenbaum.

From the documents in my possession and Simon Wiesenthal's account 'two candles for Sammy'[56] I pieced together this story that touched me deeply. At that time there were five Jewish policemen who were appointed as Kapos by the Nazis.[57] These were Farber, Sammy Frolich, Lonker, Hennek Grossbard and Joseph Grossbard. These Kapos were familiar with many of their fellow Jews and knew the staff at the school, including the Jewish girls who worked in the household of the Nazis. One of them was Ada Rawicz, nee Peller, who worked as a cleaner in the school. She became an eyewitness of the Rabka killings. After her escape she reported these to Simon Wiesenthal. Her testimony is also recorded in the trial of Wilhelm Rosenbaum and Wilhelm Oder.[58]

The Jewish family Rosenbaum had a little grocer's shop near the railway station of Rabka. The sign above the shop bore the name Stricker,[59] which was Mrs Rosenbaum's maiden name. The Rosenbaum's had two children: Paula, who was about fifteen, and Samuel, who was twelve. Samuel attended school with Mark Goldfinger whose sister Sarah Lucia was temporarily employed in the household of the camp commander, Wilhelm Rosenbaum.

Sammy's father was a tailor who lived with his family in two musty rooms and a tiny kitchen next to their little shop in Rabka. They were not rich but they were happy and

---

[56] See footnote 45

[57] The SS used Kapos (Kamp Polizei) Jewish 'policemen' to keep order among the prisoners. There were good and bad Kapos, some were sympathetic to the prisoners, other were tried after the war for crimes against their own people. See figure 15

[58] Ada Rawic was a witness at my father's war crimes trial in Linz 1948

[59] Bundesarchiv Ludwigsburg, Rosenbaum's trial (50)21/67, pp.52

religious. Every Friday night Sammy went with his father to the synagogue, after his mother and sister lit the Shabbat candles. Early afternoon one Friday in June 1942 two SS men (Wilhelm Oder & Walter Proch?) arrived at their home and arrested the Jew Rosenbaum, his wife, and their fifteen-year-old daughter Paula.

They were marched to the school where SS *Führer* Rosenbaum read through the list of arrests. The moment he spotted the identical name he suddenly beat his riding crop hard on the table and shouted, *"What is this? Rosenbaum? You dammed Jew I'll teach you a lesson for having my good German name."*

The witness said to Wiesenthal, *"we knew the Rosenbaums would be killed; it was only a matter of time. People would be executed because their name was Rosenbaum or if their first name happened to be Adolf or Hermann. The woman and the girl were marched around the schoolhouse and then I heard some shots."* [60]

When Rosenbaum discovered that the young boy of the family was missing he sent the unarmed Kapo Hennek Grossbard[61] to the stone quarry where Samuel was forced to work. [62] Mrs. Rawicz remembered Sammy Rosenbaum as *"a frail boy, with a pale, thin face and big, dark eyes, who looked much older than his age -- as did many children who learned too early about life."* [63]

Hennek Grossbard later told Ada Rawicz what happened when he went to the Zakryty stone quarry in a horse drawn cart. He stopped and waved to Sammy. Everybody in the quarry stared: the Jewish labourers and the SS guards. Sammy put down the stone he was trying to load on a truck and walked toward the cart.

---

[60] See Wiesenthal, The murderers among us, Pan Books Ltd, London, 1967, Two candles for Sammy' pp. 270

[61] His brother Josef later gave evidence against Wilhelm Rosenbaum and Wilhelm Oder

[62] Sammy was nine years old in 1939 when the Germans entered Rabka. Marek Goldfinger whom I was to meet later, remembered Sammy as a classmate who would often sit next to him in class.

[63] Simon Wiesenthal, The murderers among us, Pan Books Ltd, London, 1967, Two candles for Sammy' pp. 270

Sammy looked up at the Kapo and said. *"Where are they? Father, Mother, and Paula. Where?"* The Kapo just shook his head. Sammy understood. *"They're dead. Our name is Rosenbaum, and now you've come for me."* He stepped up and sat down next to the Kapo. The policeman had expected the boy to cry, perhaps run away. Driving out from Zakryty, he wondered how he might have forewarned the boy and allowed him to disappear in the woods where the Polish underground might have helped him. Now it was too late; the SS guards were watching.

The Kapo told Sammy what had happened that morning. Passing their house Sammy asked if they could stop for a moment. He stepped down and walked into the front room, leaving the door open. He looked over the table with the half-filled teacups left from breakfast. He looked at the clock. It was half past three. Father, Mother and Paula were already buried and no one had lit a candle for them. Slowly, methodically, Sammy cleaned off the table and put the candlesticks on it. The Kapo told Rawicz:

> *"I could see Sammy from the outside. He put on his skullcap, and lit the candles. Two for his father, two for his mother, two for his sister. And he prayed. I saw his lips moving. He said Kaddish* [64] *for them."*

Father Rosenbaum always said Kaddish for his dead parents and had taught Sammy the prayer. Now he was the only one left in his family. He stood quietly, looking at the six candles. The Jewish policeman outside saw Sammy slowly shaking his head as though he suddenly remembered something. Then Sammy placed two more candles on the table, took a match and lit them, and prayed. *"The boy knew he was already dead,"* the policeman said later. *"He lit the candles and*

---

[64] Kaddish is a Jewish prayer for the dead.

said Kaddish for himself."[65]

Samuel then climbed back on the cart where the Kapo was wiping away his tears. Samuel quietly put his hand on the man's arm to comfort him while they made their way back to the school. As they pulled up in front of the School of Murder, an SS deputy was shouting, *"Jetzt wird's aber Zeit!"* [66] Samuel was then taken into the woods behind the school and shot.[67]

This incident showed the remaining Jews that their situation was becoming hopeless. It was then that the wife of Rosenbaum Anne-Marie Bachus told Sarah Goldfinger, *"Seht zu dass ihr heute wegkommt"* ("See to it that you disappear tonight.") That night Sarah, her brother Marek and their friend Ada fled Rabka. They were some of the few who miraculously got away with the help of local Polish peasants who risked their lives to get these Jews to safety.

While Sarah managed to flee overland to Israel in 1943, Ada Rawicz survived and eventually arrived in Austria where she reported my father to the authorities at the end of the war. Wilhelm Oder was transferred to the town of Radom to head up the SD there. As the trainer of the *Einsatzgruppen* and later *Kommandeur* (KdS) of the SD, his involvement in the Holocaust was serious and undeniable.[68]

---

[65] One Friday in June, I too light a candle in memory of this courageous young man who was robbed of all his hopes and dreams, murdered in cold blood, possibly by a deluded member of my family.

[66] This was one of my father's favourite ways of expressing impatience. See glossary.

[67] In one of the court documents, my father resented the accusation by one of the witnesses, that he killed the Rosenbaum family.

[68] It is unclear how many people were murdered in Rabka. Arthur Kuhnreich Holocaust memories 1939-1945 reckoned that Rosenbaum murdered about 1000 Jews. Frania Tiger (Netzer) a Jewish survivor from Rabka testified:'The common graves contained seven times as many corpses as there were Jewish inhabitants before the war.' Robin O'Neil, the leading historian of the Rabka killing, estimates about 2000 people were murdered in Rabka. (R. O'Neil, Rabka Four: A Warning from History, Spiderwize, UK, 2011, pp. 79)

As the Nazi empire was disintegrating, especially on the eastern front, the defeat of the German Reich was becoming apparent. The rats were beginning to leave the ship and former arrogant SS members suddenly dropped their guns and ran for cover. Their fanatical *Kameradschaft* gave way to panic; it was every man for himself. When the Russians began to drive the Nazis out of Poland, my father fled with the Mauer brothers toward Austria.[69] He claimed to have been captured by the Russians, but there is no evidence for that. We know that the three killers split up on the way. The Mauer brothers fled to Salzburg, while my father arrived in Hamburg where he lived in a garden shed near his girlfriend Käthe. Not feeling secure, he left Käthe to fend for herself and her little baby girl and went into hiding in the mountains of Austria. He concealed himself near the Rettenbacher Alm, a hideout in the Austrian Dead Mountains, which was used at one time by Adolf Eichmann who had managed to escape with the help of the ODESSA[70]. From there he made his way 'home' to his family in Kremsmünster.

Surrounded by Nazi sympathisers and feeling more secure, he lost no time comforting himself with another woman, Karoline, whom he had met during one of his 'charity concerts'. Their bliss however was brief, as neither of

---

[69] See Wiesenthal, The murderers among us, Pan Books Ltd, London, 1967, page 291) the Mauer brothers were among the worst sadist of Stanislau, Poland. After their escape from Rabka they found refuge in the Evangelical Auxiliary Service (Evangelisches Hilfswerk) a charitable organisation in Salzburg, where they worked as refugee advisors and youth workers. Their arrest caused national sensation and their trial in Salzburg in 1966 resulted in anti-Semitic behaviour in the courtrooms where the defendants were applauded and the witnesses ridiculed. Their acquittal for mass murder caused demonstrations in Vienna where students held up placards reading 'Austria, National park for Nazi Criminals' (http://www.doew.at). Although they were found guilty and sentenced to 8 and 10 years prison respectively in November 1966 they were released after a short time. Austria did not like their heroes to do time in prison.

[70] See Chapter 3

them knew that Wiesenthal was on to Wilhelm Oder and that the police was already looking for him.

After having been on the run for almost three years, he was spotted and reported to the authorities by a surviving Jew who identified him as a member of the SS. At 1pm on March 4, 1948, he was arrested and placed in protective custody (to prevent anti-Nazi vigilantes from lynching and hanging him.)

Meanwhile the Polish government got wind of his arrest and applied for his extradition. They wanted to hang him for the atrocities he committed in Poland. By then the ODESSA had moved into action and used their considerable influence to get war criminals out of the country or released from jail. During the investigation Wilhelm was held in custody at an open prison in Linz, where he was given a desk job in the Hermann Göring Werke, now known as VOEST, the Austrian Steel Company. Among the privileges of a political prisoner in Austria, who looked upon war criminals as heroes and victims of 'Jewish persecution,' were visiting permits given to friends and relatives. His son Peter, who studied at the Adolf Hitler School in Steyr, was a frequent visitor, and so was Karoline. During one of Karoline's visits to the prison in the summer of 1950 I was conceived. On that Day I became the offspring of a war criminal.

Schloss Kremsegg, near Linz, Upper Austria 1951

I was born after the Second World War in the very beautiful country estate called *Schloss Kremsegg,* where my grandparents had found refuge with their three daughters.

Set on a hill 20 miles south of the city of Linz in Upper Austria, the walled Schloss Kremsegg offered a panoramic view over the nearby small town of *Kremsmünster* which is dominated by a Benedictine Monastery dating back to 777 AD.

FIGURE 16

Schloss Kremsegg

Consider then thyself and the nobility[71] within thee, for thou art honoured above all creatures, in that thou art an image of God: thou art destined for greatness.

On a sunny spring day in March 1951, the midwife slapped life into the baby boy who had arrived at a most inconvenient time, totally unplanned and largely unwanted. As a mere infant, fighting for my life with that mysterious

---

[71] Quote: Eckhart von Hochheim (Dominican Priest) 1260 - 1327

strength possessed by newborn babies, I knew nothing of those dramatic days. Coaxed into taking my first breath by the somewhat brutal methods of the day, I announced my decision to stay in the world with loud and determined cries.

Despite the shock of that first slap, the spring morning of my birth in Schloss Kremsegg was the beginning of what were to be the happiest days of my childhood. For a brief few years in the life of one born in such a dramatic and troubled period in post-war Austria, life was an enjoyable experience - eventful and full of fun. My infant memories are those of another world, one of peace and joy, a life far removed from the strange darkness that later descended and laid claim to it.

Growing up in Schloss Kremsegg, which had escaped the ravages of the war, was fabulous. The Countess employed some very interesting characters who managed the estate for her. Mr. K. was in overall charge. He was a kind hearted man, always trying to help those poor homeless souls who roamed Austria at the end of the war.

Mr. Gray was the groom. In charge of two Arab purebreds, he insisted in using them as coach horses. This they did not like, resulting in a frequent spectacle of horse and carriage racing down the roads of the estate, with the groom shouting and hanging on for dear life. From time to time the Countess would order the groom to prepare the horse team for a trip. With the 'cat' out of the house, we 'mice' enjoyed a party. Playing secretly in the chambers and rooms of the Lady of the House, we saw things that most children only dream about, imagining for a brief moment that it was we who were of royal descent. In that secret world we were kings and queens for a day.

Food for the aristocracy was provided by the cook, Mr. Small, who would daily provide high class *a-la-carte* meals for the Countess and her guests. The cook's apparel was always immaculate, his handwritten menus impeccable, his service faultless, and his food superb.

Sitting on the wall that ran around the estate, we savoured with delight the Chef's delicious dumplings, wonderful pancakes and other fine foods. From our perch we surveyed the town and villages far below, and the distant, snow-capped Alps. The air was pure and still, as though never before breathed or troubled by outside influences. Set within a land at rest after the war, the estate was a quiet and peaceful place, and its large gates, which were carefully closed at dusk, provided both privacy and security.

Miss Maria was the maid, responsible for the pigs and cows. Whenever I saw her she seemed to carry a pail of milk past the vicious cockerel who thought *he* was the owner of the estate. Every morning he would wake the estate with a loud declaration over his domain. Easily the most frightening of its residents, he defended his territory more fiercely than the gardener did his vegetable domain, with well-aimed savage pecks at innocent passers-by.

The gardener, Mr. Low, was a sinister character. He always guarded his vegetables jealously against the small intruders who devoured his sweet peas and crunchy carrots behind his back. As the former Mayor of the town he had been a fanatical Nazi during the 'occupation'. They said he was reformed and sorry for his stupidity in backing this evil regime. Appreciating the Countess' willingness to overlook his terrible past, the gardener worked hard to provide the very best for the largely self-sufficient estate which suffered little from outside food shortages. Mr. Low lived by the bottle which eventually claimed his life and that of his wife and son. He tried to forget, but no matter how much he drank he seemed unable to erase the horrors of the *Third Reich* or ease his memories.

As a little child I knew nothing of the drama that had taken place prior to my birth, nor of the confusion in the surrounding countryside. I lived for a brief moment in a little heaven on earth where the sun shone, the birds sang and the whole world of the estate was mine.

For me the freedom and the unburdened days of my early childhood were filled with peace and security which the walled estate offered. After entering the heavy cast iron gates, the drive to the *Schloss* was bordered by poplar trees that cast their shade over us during the long, hot summers as we played, rode our tricycles, or kicked a ball around.

Outside our front door was the well, with its inexhaustible supply of pure water; so refreshing to a young boy who, knowing little of the troubles that had taken place before his birth, spent his young days with little thought for what the future might hold.

We watched with fascination the frequent visitors of the Countess: highborn men and women who had escaped the traumas of war and who wasted no time in resuming their aristocratic lifestyle. From time to time relatives from the House of Habsburg, the ancient Austrian aristocracy, came to stay. They brought with them their children with whom we were occasionally permitted to play, under the strict condition that we were to address them as either "Prince" or "Princess".

Among the visitors to Schloss Kremsegg were the wealthy members of the House of Thurn und Taxis and the grandchildren of Archduke Ferdinand II, heir to the throne of the Austro-Hungarian Empire, who was assassinated in Sarajevo by murderous Serbs. The park's weeping willows were an ideal place for us to hide from the watchful eyes of the aristocrats, who wanted to be sure their children would not become contaminated by playing with us 'common children'.

Unaware of its historic connection, we roamed the estate and played wherever we liked, accompanied by the huge estate hound, a white Alsatian owned by the manager. 'Wurli' was our pet, our friend and our guard - no one dared approach the children he watched over obediently.

Chapter 3

The reality of our situation was, however, very different. We were not the owners of the Schloss, though I was often given the impression that it was 'ours'. Unfortunately, our idyllic surroundings were not to last; our dream came to an end. Unnoticeably, storm clouds gathered on the horizon. Soon our dreams of a bright future turned into our worst nightmares.

Though the power of the Nazis was broken, they were far from defeated. Many escaped with riches that their evil empire had robbed from the victims of their crimes. (From the beginning, the Nazis forced the Jews to pay 147.5 million Reichark as 'Jewish wealth tax' besides 181 million in taxes for leaving the country. From Austrian Jews alone the Nazis stole at least 5,000 million Schillings (about 250 million Pounds Sterling).

The Secrets of the ODESSA

With the hidden wealth and gold stolen from the countless millions who were plundered and murdered, ex-members of the Gestapo, the SS and other officials of Hitler's murderous regime financed the ODESSA. ODESSA does not stand for the Ukrainian city on the shores of the Black Sea. ODESSA is an acronym for *Organisation Der Ehemaligen SS Angehörigen* (organisation of former members of the SS[72]), who reportedly aided Nazis to hide or escape to foreign shores where they would be safe from prosecution.

Though the ODESSA[73] was never officially organised, it functioned very effectively for many years after the war. It consisted of sympathisers from all walks of life within post-

---

[72] In my childhood I heard of this organisation, which was sometimes called 'Die Spinne' – (the spider), due to the widespread web of conspiracy. This author also knows of secret sympathisers in Austria today who would, given the opportunity, aid and abet Nazi war criminals at a moment's notice.

[73] Uki Goni, The Real ODESSA, Uki Goni, Granta Books, London (2002)

war Europe who were still committed to the cause of Nazi Germany. After the war Austria, yet again, provided amnesty for over 10,000 convicted war criminals and reinstated 4,000 other Nazis, among them judges, lawyers, policemen and politicians, to public offices. Quietly resuming their pre-war roles, they did nothing to eliminate their nation's ingrained anti-Semitism, but supported the secret network of the ODESSA. Austria was never denazified. If anything, Austria was called the *National Park for Nazi Criminals* after the war.

During the 1983 elections in Austria it came to light that the man who ran for the presidential office, Dr. Kurt Waldheim, had been a member of the SA, Hitler's paramilitary 'street gang' (something Waldheim, typical Austrian, denied). Former World Jewish Congress executive director Elan Steinberg, a key player in a campaign against Waldheim that ended with his being barred from the United States, said, *"The sad thing is that he could not confront the truth even at the end. Now he is before God and cannot lie."* [74] Man's greatest fear is being confronted with the truth about himself. Many of these former members and officials of Hitler's ruling party escaped justice and mysteriously came into riches after the war, often quite blatant about their rank and activity during the war. Policemen known to have belonged to the Gestapo were especially respected. Lawyers and businessmen who knew one another as former *Kameraden* received preferential treatment. Most of them soon regained positions of influence in both politics and government. Scores of the Ex-SS *Angehörigen* formed themselves into a party that was powerful enough to make deals with the weak post-war Austrian government; it was largely the ODESSA which was behind the *Verein der Unabhängigen (VDU)*, the Neo-Nazi Independence Party of 1953.

---

[74] holycoast.blogspot.com/.../former-un-chief-austrian-leader-kurt.html

In 1954 they made a secret pact with the Austrian ruling party, the Volkspartei (Austrian People's Party), where they pressured the Government into withholding *Wiedergutmachung* (compensation) from the Jews and divert it to their cause:

The Independence Party demands that the total wealth of heirless Jews is to be used as a compensation for those who were forced to return requisitioned Jewish properties.[75]

Imagine the gall and audacity of this band of fanatics who demanded compensation for giving up the property they stole from their murdered victims. When dealing with Nazis you deal with devils!

ODESSA influenced many top lawyers, officials and politicians to favour their colleagues, with the result that many were acquitted. Under false names hundreds were able to start a new life in parts of the world far from the vengeance-seeking survivors of Nazi extermination camps.

This organisation was made up of a large number of volunteers who used any means to rescue their heroes. One of the most controversial routes became known as the *Convent Route* (or *Monastary Route*) which used monasteries and convents in which to hide Nazis.

ODESSA's Monastery Escape Route

One member of the ODESSA who used the Convent Route was another Catholic Church leader, Dr *Alois Hudal*, who considered Hitler as 'Siegfried of German greatness' [76]. Hudal was one of those who, in their delusion, established the *Convent Route* to aid the escape of Nazi war criminals.

As an Austrian, Hudal was Dean of the national German Catholic Church in Rome and bishop of *Santa Maria del' Anima*. He openly admitted in his published *Roman Diary* that he was proud to have devoted his total ministry to the former members of the NS regime and particularly to the so-called

---

[75] Josef Fraenkel, The Jews of Austria, Vallentine Mitchell & Co. Ltd. London, 1967, Gustav Jellinek, Die Geschichte der Österreichischen Wiedergutmachung, pp.410(Par.8 pp.3)

[76] Ernst Klee, Persilscheine und falsche Pässe. Wie die Kirchen den Nazis halfen (Whitewash Certificates and False Passports. How the Churches Helped the Nazis), Frankfurt, Fischer Geschichte,1991

war criminals who he considered to be unfairly persecuted by Communists and 'Christian' democrats. Hudal's 'ministry' provided shelter, food and clothing while the Italian Red Cross issued identification papers that were stamped by the Argentinean Immigration Commission in Genoa.

This deluded man religiously prayed for the mass murderers, *"I thank the Lord that he opened my eyes and granted me the undeserving gift…to console many victims - by means of false ID papers - having torn quite a few of them from the grasp of their tormentors for escape into happier lands."*[77]

One of those who escaped to the happier land of Egypt was Aribert Heim, who was known as 'Dr. Death' in Buchenwald and Mauthausen. There he tortured people to death, like Mengele, with horrific medical experiments. With his new identity and the help of the ODESSA, Aribert Heim safely lived in Cairo as Tarek Hussein Farid until his death in 1992.

---

[77] Zvi Aharoni and Wilhelm Dietl, Operation Eichmann, Cassel Military Paperbacks, Cassel & Co, 1996, pp. 54

FIGURE 18

65

The Trial

While the ODESSA[78] did not manage to enable my father to escape from Austria, they managed to make his war trial a 'success'. From documents in my possession I have evidence that 'the spider' provided positive character reference through at least three witnesses who were probably paid off by a leading ODESSA member of this author's family. In the poverty of post-war Austria, it will have been very tempting for starving people to receive money, accommodation, and food in return for making positive statements. This was a well-established principle in post-war Austria, where as many as 17,000 people were guilty of crimes against humanity. To neutralise accusations against people on trial, the ODESSA provided judges and lawyers who were sympathetic to the cause of the Nazis.

Often the leader of the jury was a well known Nazi. In many trials, eye witnesses were openly ridiculed and blatantly intimidated. Volunteers who came forward with mitigating evidence, such as positive character references, were given priority. No doubt they were rewarded. In my father's trial it seemed enough for the defence to repeat statements saying that *"Wilhelm Oder was a good man"*, *"the best of the Germans,"* [79] in order to shift the attention away from his crimes. Providing positive character evidence at my father's war crime trial, which took place in the Nazi stronghold of Linz, effectively neutralised his accusers and turned the case in his favour. Witnesses such as Roman D., Karl P., Franciszek M. were probably bribed to provide positive character references. Rosenbaum, himself accused of murder, questioned these later at his trial: *"On orders from me Oder always participated in the execution of Jews without any qualms. I don't*

---

[78] The ODESSA stage-managed many of the trials such as the trial of the Mauer brothers in Salzburg where the leader of the Jury was a former member of the Sturm Abteilung (SA), Hitler's terrorist street gangs.

[79] Franciszek M, war crime document 157, in author's possession

know why some witnesses want to protect him."[80]

The author has documents that show the powerful influence of the ODESSA which also effectively blocked the extradition requested by the Polish government who wanted to try my father on Polish soil.[81] One particular female supporter offered to provide mitigating evidence for my father. On June 7, 1948, she sent a secret message suggesting to exchange documents with my father's brother in a clandestine meeting point in the Bavarian mountains:

Would it be possible for you to take some time off [from work] for us to meet at the Schumacherkreuz [cross placed on top of a mountain], which runs right across the border? I would travel to Reit im Winkel [village straddling Austrian/German border] and climb up to the Hindenburg Hütte. The Austrian Chalet is on the Eggen Alm on the Austrian side...

This letter is being transported in the same way. Do you think you or your brother [ranking ODESSA member] could do this? You only need to send a card with the date on which you will be at the Schumacherkreuz.[82]

---

[80] Bundesarchiv, Ludwigsburg, Rosenbaum trial, statement 141 Js 856/61, pp. 2.572/2.573
[81] Ibid 6AR-Z34/61 pp. 6/217
[82] Translated from original German document in the author's possession. Explanatory comments in brackets are mine.

FIGURE 19

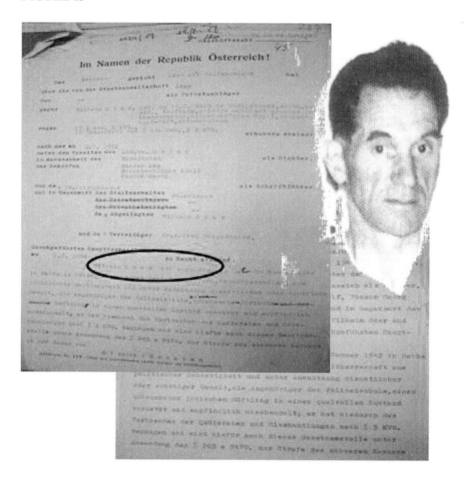

Never before was our earthly home exposed to the political and physical challenges we are facing today. Never before did man give such high tribute to nature, while seeing himself utterly vulnerability in the face of destructive forces, he himself has brought about. [83]

---

[83] Michail Gorbatschow, Report at the communist party-political Congress, February 25, 1986

Though found guilty on the account of unlawful wounding and mistreatment of a prisoner, the rest of his indictments were thrown out as 'insufficient evidence', despite the eyewitness accounts. He was sentenced to a mere six months of hard labour.

During the investigation and court proceedings he was held in a remand prison in Linz where other war criminals were awaiting trial. One of them was the Commander of Treblinka concentration camp, the Austrian Franz Stangl. Stangl, one of those mysterious people coming from Upper Austria who seemed to have this inbred panache for anti-Semitism and cold blooded murder. After serving as a Gestapo Agent in Linz, he was put in charge of Sobibor and Treblinka extermination camps, where he was promoted to 'the best commandant' in Poland for his services to the Reich. Between 1941-1943, he was responsible for the murder of approximately 900,000 people. In 1948, he was spirited away from Linz and managed to escape to Brazil with the help of Catholic priest Alois Hudal who provided him with an international identity card from the Red Cross[84] (possibly paid for by Hudal's secret Church funds.)

---

[84] Thanks to Simon Wiesenthal's dogged detective work, Stangl was arrested on February 28, 1967. On December 22, 1970 he was found guilty of the murder of 1200000 people and sentenced to life imprisonment. He died of heart failure a year later.

FIGURE 20

Man's greatest fear is to be confronted with the truth about himself. [85]

---

[85] Werner Oder

God promised Abraham that he would be a blessing to all the nations of the world. Since Abraham was the founder and patriarch of the Jewish nation, God's intent was for the Jews to be a blessing to the whole world. It had less to do with who they were, but more with who their God was. He chose to be known as the God of Abraham, purely because He made Himself known to Abraham. Because Abraham was singled out for this, he came under God's special protection:

I will bless those who bless you and whoever curses you I will curse. (Genesis 12:3)

The Nazis in general and my ancestors in particular cursed the Jews. Because of this the curse of God came upon us. Though these scriptures are often used as a warning, very few people know what the curse was or how it manifested. Though Abraham received these prophecies, the world had to wait 400 years until Moses defined them in Deuteronomy chapter 28. The first 14 verses speak about the blessings; the remaining 54 verses describe the horror of the curse in detail.

Verse 20 begins with 'The Lord will send on you curses, confusion and rebuke ... plague you with diseases ... strike you with fever and inflammation ... cause you to be defeated ... afflict you with tumours and madness, blindness and confusion of mind ... give you a fearful mind ... terror will fill your heart ... The sky over your head will be bronze ... you will live inconstant suspense, filled with dread both night and day...'

This became our daily lot. We lived under the curse day and night; there was no relief. *'These curses will come upon you and overtake you until you are destroyed'.*[86]

My brother Wilhelm died without God in a trench far from home, crying for his mother. He gave his life for the

---

[86] Deuteronomy 28:45 NIV

insanity of the Hitler youth after being indoctrinated by the likes of SS Chief Heinrich Himmler who addressed them saying:

The German youth have learned once again to value people racially...they have turned away once again from the Christian theory, from the Christian teachings which ruled Germany for more than a thousand years...and almost caused its racial death... [87]

My other half-brother Peter [88] had immigrated to Australia in an attempt to get away from the demons that haunted him. Peter and I were very close, both in personality and suffering. Between the lines of his letters I read the struggles, the pain of his effort to come to terms with his/our legacy. Though he never divulged what he heard during the trial of father, the secret shame and horror was slowly destroying him. We often talked on the phone trying to carry each other's burden. Because at that time I struggled with the horror of my psychological heritage myself, I was unable to help him. As I watched, I realised that my brother was slowly dying inside. The love he longed to receive from father never came, even though he tried to be reconciled during a brief visit to Austria.

Returning to Australia a deeply disillusioned man, his marriage began to fail. With that, the little flame of hope

---

[87] Williamson Gordon: Hitler's Instrument of terror, Sidgwick & Jackson, London, 1995, pp. 101

[88] Picture of my older brothers Wilhelm and Peter in Hitler Youth Uniform

began to flicker. In a vain effort to help my dying brother, I tried to reach out to him, tried to be the brother who felt as he felt, only to see him fade from my life. He was unable to come to terms with 'the legacy' which was destroying his soul. He soon died of leukaemia far from home and far from his family.

When I received the news of his sudden death, I felt an icy grip on my heart. I was reminded again of the cost of being the son of a Nazi war criminal.

My oldest half sister, the child of Wilhelm Rosenbaum's Secretary Käthe Engelmann, struggles to live with the legacy of her heritage. My other sister is unable to talk about the man they said was her father. I cannot tell their stories; I can only tell my story and my battle with sickness, dread and despair which became my constant companions as a result of the evil legacy my father left us. The curse of anti-Semitism rested upon our home; it was a home without God, without joy or purpose.

A few hours after the trial, my father was released from prison in February 1952. He lost no time in removing his family from the heaven of Schloss Kremsegg to the hell of two very small and vermin infested rooms without sanitation. From the day we moved it seemed as if someone switched off the light as darkness descended upon our home. Even now half a century later, I remember clearly the day we moved out of light into darkness. From that day demonic forces invaded my home and turned my days into a fearful existence amidst the quarrels of my parents.

FIGURE 21

She dreamt of a bright future, while he tried to hide his past. [89]

Visions of Hell

The nightmares started the day father moved in with us. I remember them clearly as if they happened yesterday. It was not just the odd nightmare a child occasionally has. These were repeated nightmares which varied in intensity and

---

[89] Ibid

frequency.

I woke up sensing that someone was in my room. A terrible fear gripped my heart and I cringed in my bed, helplessly paralyzed by what was happening. Although the room was dark I could see the ground like a tomb from which a horrific looking creature appeared. His horned head, pointed ears sometimes laid flat as that of a mad cat, a revolting face like a goat covered with matted red hair. He was evil beyond description, rising up from an opening in the ground that was like a grave. He turned his head toward me, leered at me with merciless, cold eyes that were dead. He approached me slowly.

At first I was paralyzed with terror, and then I screamed and screamed. Mother came rushing into the room expecting the worst. At her appearance the sneering visage withdrew and returned to its hole in the ground, leaving me quivering and hysterical. I was too small to say what I had seen, much less explain what I had experienced.

Having no idea of what the problem was, Mother did her best to calm me, but even had she known what had taken place she would have been helpless against the evil monster that had come to claim her firstborn son. She did her best to calm her little boy. When she went back to bed I wrapped myself into my quilt for protection. Eventually I fell into a fitful sleep. But the next night the nightmares started again. And the following night. Night after night with rarely a break.

To give her a break, my mother would sometimes take me to her parents at Schloss Kremsegg for a day or two. There the sun always seemed to shine; I felt safely out of reach of this monster.

Yet returning to the slums we called home, the nightly 'visits' continued. Each nightly attack was followed by personal health problems. My parents' domestic grievances and the neighbourhood conflicts were systematically destroying my young life. Rarely was there a night when I could rest; rarely a day when I enjoyed being alive.

FIGURE 22

One falsehood creates a thousand fears.[90]

I tried to talk to my parents about the nightmares and showed them where the devil kept appearing from a hole in the living room floor. But because there was nothing that could be seen, they chided me for being so stupid. No one listened to me or cared. I tried to forget but that was too difficult. I tried and tried to tell Mother, but she thought I'd had another bad dream that would go away.

But it did not go away; neither did *he*. He enjoyed his nightly visits. Returning time and time again, he would stop at the side of my bed and stare into my terrified face.

---

[90] African saying

Sometimes I would hear nothing but his footsteps by my bedside. At other times he would reach out his hand toward me and I would recoil in absolute horror at the thought of his touch. I wanted to flee from this evil presence - to run to my father or hide in mother's arms. Strangely, father was never about. I longed for his protection while at the same time I was afraid of him. He seemed cold hearted and careless. I longed for his protection from these nightly onslaughts that drove me to the end of my sanity. Night after night for almost five years I lived in terror of the dark. One particular nightmare was so horrific that I can remember its details to this day. Now many decades later, at any given moment, no matter where I am, I can close my eyes and recall this event:

I awoke as something like a clawed hand closed around my throat. He was there. Slowly tightening his grip on my chest until I could no longer breathe, much less scream. I struggled and fought hard to get him off me, to loosen his iron grip, but to no avail. I felt myself slipping into unconsciousness, dropping into endless darkness. I could hear distant echoes of a child screaming. I was falling, falling deeper into the shadows of another world.

Then someone was shaking me; familiar voices were calling my name from far away. I was spinning through an unknown world. The dim light was receding faster and faster, amid fading voices that seemed like ethereal sounds from another world. Drawn by unknown powers I felt heavier and heavier, aware that ugly fears from unknown spheres rode along like darting shadows.

Strange echoes were calling me, even while unfamiliar sounds pounded my mind. Beneath me I could see a great blackness, almost like a giant mouth, and I was travelling toward it at a great speed. *"No."* I screamed, *"Noooo..."*

I heard voices asking questions in a confusing cacophony of sounds. At the same time a question was forming slowly, very slowly, in my mind: *"Where am I, where is this journey taking me?"*

Suddenly I stopped falling and began to ascend away from the darkness toward the light, feeling an increasing lightness in my body. I heard the voices again, closing in on me, getting louder and louder. I began to sense familiar surroundings and felt something cool touch my chest, then my forehead. I opened my eyes to see tired eyes behind the rimmed spectacles of a man I knew only as 'Uncle Doctor.' Behind him I recognized the tearstained face of my mother; she was calling my name. I barely had the strength to ask *"Mother, am I going to die?"*

While 'Uncle Doctor' gravely continued with whatever he was doing, Mother sobbed a quiet, *"No, my child, you are just very sick."*

I made a slow recovery, observing from my bed the increasing sadness of a mother whose 'dream' marriage was falling apart. Comforting herself with constant cigarettes, she had also begun to drink.

All this time my father was out 'visiting'. They said he was trying to get a job. Most likely he was just visiting his many lady friends. At any rate he needed to be away from the pressure of a home in the slums and the sickness of his son. Whenever I heard him come home I tried to get up for him, so I could be with the one I loved to call 'father'.

As a hard, former SS soldier, he was brainwashed with the delusions of Aryan health and strength. He had no time at all for the weak or the sick. Rather, they should not be permitted to live, for in his world only the strong survived. On those rare occasions when he was home I tried my hardest to oblige him, but to no avail.

The following week I had recovered enough to play outside, still feeling the effects of what had happened and wondering what kind of world I had entered during the lowest point of my illness. I could only sit quietly on my chair outside and gaze thoughtfully at the distant mountains, trying to work out what was happening to me. Why was I here? Why could I not go back and live at the Schloss where the sun shone and the birds sang?

When my sister came along, mother reached breaking point. Besides grappling with the demands of a very small family, she had to cope with the increasingly absent husband. Lack of finance and a sick child added to her misery of loneliness and emotional pain. Her only comfort was to visit her friends in the evening after she put her children to bed. Unfortunately her children did not stay asleep but woke all too often, finding the house dark and empty with no parents in sight. Crying in distress, we wandered about the dark streets in search of mother. As this was in the days before the event of the telephone, it usually took some time for compassionate neighbours to send word: *"your children are wandering about the neighbourhood screaming, again."*

Other times, less compassionate people who knew that Mrs. Oder had left her children alone at home would sneak up and tap on our windows, making scary noises. Their perverted sense of humour seemed to get a kick out of terrorising small children who felt scared to death. Eventually mother returned with alcohol on her breath, chiding us for our behaviour and for getting out of bed. Yet in her own way we knew she loved us, even though it seemed as if no one else loved her, except her father who all too soon died a broken man.

The Night I Wished I Died

Jesus asked the boy's father, 'How long has he been like this?' 'From childhood,' he answered. 'The demon has often thrown him into the fire or water to kill him.' [91]

It was while I was playing outside that *he* struck, unexpectedly. I did not see him coming; nor did I have my

---

[91] Matthew 9:21 NIV

usual sense of foreboding. I remember only that all of a sudden a great pain tore through my body. It felt as if I was lifted into the air from the side of a large, concrete water tank by an unseen force. My horrified scream was cut short by the impact of my body on water that was so cold it numbed me all over. The shock of freezing water closed over me, taking my breath. Despite thrashing desperately, I began to sink. As I sank to the bottom of the tank, my cries were muffled by water rushing into my lungs. The sound of air bubbles leaving my mouth was accompanied by cries of pain; my fingers clawed at the side of the algae-covered concrete walls.

Black and red visions from hell began whirling through my mind, mixed with the blurred image of a neighbour's horrified face that appeared suddenly above the surface. While passing by he had heard the frantic splashing and was able to reach down and pull me out. Having no knowledge of first aid procedures, he simply tipped me upside down to allow the water to drain from my lungs and then pummelled me until I started breathing again. I felt the now warm water leave my lungs and then was carried, coughing and spluttering, to our nearby home. There I was cared for by my panic-stricken mother who was informed that someone had found me at the bottom of a water tank.

It was spoken of as 'a bad accident': *"he must have fallen in"*. *"Forget it"*, I was told, but how could I forget the strange experience of inhaling a large amount of water, the slow sense of suffocation, the fading light, and the evil grimace on a haunting face?

There was no one I could tell, or at least no one who was interested; all were so busy with their own survival. Life was hard and hatred was rife. In our area the hunt was on for war criminals. Local soldiers were returning from prisoner-of-war camps in Russia, bedraggled and broken. Many of them had walked halfway across war-torn Europe, abused along the way by those they had abused. Former concentration camp inmates were telling their stories to a generally unbelieving population, who *'knew nothing, saw nothing and'* of course *'did nothing.'*

Jewish survivors of the extermination camps were beginning their work of revenge: ejecting from their homes the Nazis who had stolen them, submitting compensation forms, and hunting down former SS thugs. Every day the Red Cross radio broadcast the names of those still missing. Amid the devastation a sad and confused world had no room for a sick child who was, after all, in the care of his parents. So many had died or been injured or permanently disabled, so why worry about a child who had fallen into a water tank? It had been an accident. These things happen.

And at night *he* was back again. His onslaught was relentless. I was trying desperately to get away - to run, hide. But that was in my dream. In reality I was thrashing on my bed, fighting for oxygen and crying in terror as a huge weight seemed to settle on my chest.

I pleaded with this monster, begging him to leave me alone, promising that I would do anything if only he would. But he never spoke to me and never let up. The accidents and nightmares continued. Four or five times I was thrown into water and had to be rescued. One time I was thrown down a flight of concrete stairs and landed on my face. From this accident alone I received injuries that caused people to stop and stare at me in horror. After other terrible falls I received back and spinal injuries that trouble me to this day.

When I started school I discovered that I loved learning to read and to write. But it was difficult for me to enjoy school life. Although our school was not ruled by the proverbial law of the jungle, the unwritten law of the survival of the fittest was very much the order of the day. Unable to defend myself physically or to command respect in other ways, I soon found the nightmare of home blending with the nightmare of schooldays. Unable to participate in the school's activities, I became a loner, missing most lessons through doctor's appointments and hospital visits. So weak was I that even though our home was almost next door to the school, I was often unable to walk the few yards between them.

One cold, winter morning, a thick blanket of snow covered the ground and the windows of our small flat were iced up. After a night of watching the endless quarrelling of my parents and nightmares to follow, I found myself unable to breathe. My head was pounding from lack of oxygen. I asked my father for help. After telling me to grab my school satchel, he pushed me roughly out the door, saying, *"All you need is some fresh air."* To him only the strong were worthy of life; the weak and sickly were a burden to society and so were 'surplus to requirement.'

Lacking the strength to walk and having no coat to protect me from the outside temperature, which was way below freezing, I hid behind some snowdrifts and waited until I saw my father leave the house. Mother, who had watched me fearfully, ushered me quickly back inside, doing her best to help her sickly son even while desperately needing help herself. For mother there was no friend to call upon and no God to cry to for help. She had a husband who did not love her and I had a father who did not care. He soon left mother for yet another woman, abandoning us, as he did the children of his previous relationships. The curse was an awful reality that dominated our home:

> *The Lord will send fearful plagues on you and your descendants, harsh and prolonged diseases and severe lingering illnesses.*[92]

Both my grandparents died of *severe lingering illnesses.* I was suffering from *prolonged diseases* from childhood. The pain that wracked my body from morning till night screamed out for

---

[92] Deuteronomy 28:59 NIV

justice, for freedom from the monster, understanding from my teachers, acceptance from my peers, and love from my parents. Inside me something had began to simmer. At first too insignificant to be noticed, but as the years advanced it became clear that a thing dark and strange was beginning to occupy my mind - a burning hatred. Hatred of this world, of our helplessness, of injustice, of the disabilities that imprisoned me in a life I had not chosen; a society that had no time for the sick and the infirm and a world that was not fair. I became a very angry young man. I wanted to get even, kill and destroy everything and everyone who prevented me from living.

The Lord will afflict you with madness and confusion of mind. [93]

Darkness covered my mind and insane feelings began to control my life. I found it increasingly difficult to differentiate from the world around me and the fearful world that existed in my mind. Unable to enjoy the good in life, I began to enjoy its dark side. Growing out of childhood without maturing in mind and body, I began to experiment with alcohol in a bid to drown my sorrows and drink up the courage to stay alive another day.

Suicide

Whatever I tried in self-help, it did not seem to deal with the deep-seated inner turmoil that was ravaging my soul. *'The sky over your head will be bronze.'* [94]

I wanted the trouble to end and began to think about committing suicide. If that is what life was all about, I did not want it; there was no hope, no help and no one to care. I decided to end it all. Taking hold of my mother's biggest box of pills, I quickly swallowed them all and hurried to my

[93] Ibid Verse 28
[94] Deuteronomy 28:23 NIV

favourite place in the woods. Expecting to lose consciousness any moment, I carved my name, time and date into a tree and sat down to await the end.

I had no regrets and no thought what heartache my action would provoke, I just wanted to die and get rid of the living hell of fear and pain. Hour after hour went by; it grew dark. And still I experienced no effects from the overdose. Night fell as I sat alone and contemplated my fate. Oddly, I was beginning to feel happy in myself. Things were not that bad I thought. As the night wore on I was beginning to feel strangely elated and somewhat lightheaded. Since life did not seem so bad after all, I decided to go home. It felt as if I was walking on air, which was very puzzling since I was supposed to die. But dying was far from my mind which was suddenly soaring with unaccustomed happiness. Despite the darkness of the night, there were bright colours everywhere. I felt weightless, carefree and light. Grinning and laughing at the shadows, I stumbled through the woods. No demons, fears or pain. This was good; this was what I was looking for. This must be heaven.

But it did not last and... I did not die, though I should have. The dose was enough to kill. (The mystery was resolved much later when my mother discovered she had run out of her tranquilizers, though she was sure that there was a spare box somewhere.) Needless to say this strange happiness soon gave way to the old depressions, before long I was back in the bottom of the pit.

Increasingly rejected by society, I began to seek out those of like mind - other rejects. I found myself enjoying the company of those who held no particular beliefs, who respected no one in general, and who had no moral values. The good was our enemy; the bad became our friend.

The crime and vandalism that resulted gave me the 'buzz' I needed. Like so many frustrated youngsters I vented my anger on the cars and property of those who, unlike me, had 'made it' in life. I soon became known to those on the fringe of society as a 'madman' and to the police as a 'known person'. I was spiralling out of control.

As well as being sick in body, I was sick in mind. Often I found it difficult to distinguish between the reality I did not want to face and the fantasies I tried so hard to chase. Life must have been hell for my poor mother who was unable to care for a son who was at war with anyone or anything that stood in his way. The spirit of hatred and anti-Semitism had made its home in my soul. I was lost in a world of evil I could not control.

Brought up on extreme racial prejudice and anti-Semitic hatred, it was normal for me to consider Jews as inferior to us, the supposed 'Aryan super race'. Even as a child I knew that soap was apparently made from the bones of the Jews. I heard about lamp shades being made from the skin of Jews. It was all part of my phraseology and I understood the concepts, heard the racial abuse and knew about the terrible prejudice against 'dirty Jews.'

Yet amid this great turmoil I managed to finish high school, to the great relief of my teachers who all agreed on one thing: *"If this boy ever becomes something, we'll take our hats off to him."*

I did not know anything about God. I did not know who He was and where He was. Our home was godless, remember? All I knew was that there was a kind of Santa Claus 'up there' who watched our struggles without lifting a hand to help. Strangely though I discovered that during one of my scream-filled nightmares I had started to pray. I prayed a prayer that no one ever taught me. (Shortly before her death my mother told me that one night she had overheard me pray. She was so touched by that prayer that she wrote it on a slip of paper.) Somehow this prayer in the godless home of her Nazi husband struck a chord in her soul:

Dear God, look upon me your little child and have mercy on my tears. I do not want to die. If you let me live I will serve you.

I have often puzzled over this prayer. How come I prayed this since I had no knowledge of God whatsoever? Where did this prayer come from? I had no idea where, what or who God was. Yet it appears that from the bottom of my heart I cried out to 'someone', even though he appeared to be far, far away. Having prayed the prayer, it seemed at first as if there was no answer. Without any sign of improvement in my physical or mental health I spent most of my life curled up in bed. Like a frightened animal I hid from the evils that were destroying my life. My body was twisted out of shape. Unable to eat I became too weak to play outside. The presents I received on my birthdays brought little joy into my world of horror, pain and illness. With the unanswered prayer fading and the dread of death spreading in my mind, I began to despair of life. Yet somewhere, far away, there was this mysterious glimmer of hope that maybe, one day, I would be saved from pain and delivered from all evil.

Out of Control

I celebrated leaving school by getting drunk and going out looking for fights. A strange dark force had spread in my soul. I wanted to kill anyone who stood in my way. I used phrases my father used when he was angry with many of the foreign immigrants from the east: *"Ich werde das G'sindl über'n Haufen schießen"* ("I will shoot these vagrants into a pile [of bodies]").

This kind of behaviour escalated, even during my apprenticeship. The staff of the company that had employed me found themselves unable to help or control this generally insubordinate and unteachable youngster. During the day I managed to put on a tough face, but during the night I was really scared; it was during the night that the visitors from hell still terrorized me. I needed help and secretly hoped for someone to come and help me. No one did and no one could. The doctors could not. Neither could the teachers, the police or the social workers.

I wanted to be accepted and loved, but the more I tried to be acceptable the more rejection I felt. I did not know it then but know now that I was under a curse I could not shake off. I seemed to vacillate between being manic depressive and flying into white rage when confronted with injustice. This personality disorder caused tremendous instability, diverting me onto a path of wanting to do evil for the smallest injustice. I would sit down and plan to kill this one and that one simply because they crossed me. The curse of Nazi death cult spread in my heart, the curse of having a father who was a terrorist and a killer.

Chapter 4

A Ray of Hope

Unbeknown to me however God had not forgotten my prayer but had heard the cry of that traumatised child who cried out to Him from the bottom of the pit. Seven years had passed since I prayed the prayer; I was still alive, though enduring a troubled existence. That was about to change. In what seemed an answer to my prayer, God called a German to become a missionary to the young people of Austria. Obedient to his calling, Peter made his way over the mountains into Austria to start a work among the deprived youth of post-war-Austria. When I met Peter I had no idea who he was or why he was here, yet meeting him had a great unsettling effect upon my life. He fixed his clear brown eyes on me and said:

> *Werner, God loves you so much that He gave His only Son to die for you on the cross. If you ask your heavenly father to forgive your sins and give your life to Jesus, he will forgive you all your sin and heal all your pain. Call upon the name of the Lord and He will set you free.*

I could not believe my ears. This man talked about knowing God, about Him being my heavenly father who loved me, about being set free and forgiven. Could this God deal with the darkness and hatred in my soul? I went away deeply disturbed, trying to understand, believe and hope. For three days I wrestled, unable to rest, hoping desperately that what this man told me was true. Then, on the third day, I decided to put the whole thing to the test. After further instructions by Peter I decided to put my trust in God.

Freedom from the Curse

Determined to believe that Jesus Christ redeemed me from the curse by becoming a curse for me, I pleaded with God to bless me. I decided to believe in the God of Israel who sent His Son Jesus to become Israel's Messiah and the Saviour of the world. I believed that He had the power and was willing to forgive me and deliver me from the curse that made life hell for me.

When I fell to my knees to surrender my life to Christ I was unprepared for what was about to take place. Kneeling to confess my sin and my need of forgiveness and deliverance, it seemed as if the weight of the whole world rolled off my shoulders. With tears forming in my eyes, I sensed the light of God flooding my mind, driving out the darkness of despair and fear. Like chains, the troubles of my soul fell off; my sanity returned to me. I knew from that moment that God's only Son Jesus Christ had come to set this prisoner free.

I was no longer alone but felt deeply loved and somehow highly favoured. I believed that I had become a child of the eternal God who had come to set me free from all evil. He had responded to my prayer and I knew that God was real and He was alive and powerful. From that day, all demons left and my nightmares stopped. From that day, the darkness in my life vanished to give way to the eternal rays of hope that led me to discover Jesus Christ as my Messiah who had come to set me free from the demons of hell and the curse of the evil empire of Nazi Germany.

The miraculous freedom from the curse did not come about through some imaginary trick of the mind or any religious figment of the imagination. Like a fly in the spider's web, I was unable to free myself from the power of the curse. When I believed in Jesus Christ, I experienced His power delivering me from the curse. A rabbi from Tarsus experienced this freedom in an even greater way. He wrote about it in 35 AD:

> *Christ redeemed us from the curse of the law by becoming a curse for us, for it is written: "Cursed is everyone who is hung on a tree." He redeemed us in order that the blessing given to Abraham might come to the Gentiles through Christ Jesus, so that by faith we might receive the promise of the Spirit.*[95]

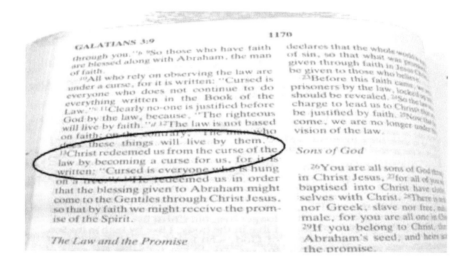

Just like the psalmist, I experienced the righteousness of the Lord *'cutting me free from the cords of wickedness.'*[96]

No ancestral cords, hereditary sin, generational curses remained in place; it was for freedom that Christ had set me free. I was free indeed and no deliverance seminar or inner healing conference could add to this freedom. Christ had done it all and his work was finished and complete. He broke the curse and set me free.

---

[95] Galatians 3:13 NIV
[96] Psalm 129:4 NIV

Returning from this life-changing moment where Heaven opened its windows to this troubled young man, my witness to the saving power of Christ was met with stony silence at home. Soon my newly found freedom was contested by the dismay and consternation of family and friends who thought it unacceptable that an Aryan should profess faith in this Jesus Christ. A Jew! My testimonies to the power of God's Grace soon attracted violent reactions and vehement opposition, accusing me of fanaticism, of being a Jew-lover and worse.

With God's supernatural courage, my newly found faith soon turned into a battle that taught me to fight the good fight of faith. I also began to understand the reality of faith where many believers were sent to the death camps. Had I been born earlier and come to Christ during the fascist regime that murdered pastors and priest in the camps of hell, they would have sent me to the camps.

Undeterred, I allowed nothing and no one to stop me following the Lord. He had saved me from sin and delivered me from the jaws of despair and distress. Since the nightmares stopped on the day I trusted in Christ the Messiah, no one could shake my faith and I allowed no one to steal my joy or my newly found freedom. But there were new forces arrayed against me. I had no idea of where the battle lines were drawn and how to fight an enemy I could not see. In the past I had learned how to take care of myself, but this kind of warfare was different. I had to learn how to fight the good fight of faith.

FIGURE 23

Nothing is easier than to denounce the evil doer, nothing is more difficult than to understand him. [97]

While I was serving my term in the military, I received the news of the death of my father. It had been well over

---

[97] Fyodor Dostoyevsky, Russian Novelist 1821-1881

fifteen years since I last saw him.

Wiesenthal had collected new evidence against my father who was facing a retrial. This time the ODESSA was unable to help him due to scandalous trials that had shaken Austria's judicial system in the past. This time there would be no escape; father was facing a possible life sentence. The prospect of being tried again terrified him. Upon receiving the court orders in 1970, his heart failed him. He died suddenly at the age of 65.

I stood beside his open coffin, looking at the face of a man who was supposed to be my father. Surrounded by some of his former comrades, I stared at the gaunt features of a stranger, the father I never knew. I felt no emotions. As far as I was concerned he never played a major part in my life. He left us many years ago, after which he never enquired as to the welfare of his children or assisted his former wife in raising them. He abandoned us as he did all the other women and the children he fathered. I felt no hatred for him yet sensed a strange pang of regret for never knowing him.

As the clods of earth fell upon the coffin, I realised that this was the final contact with the man they said was my father. The chapter of a fatherless childhood was closed. I wanted to say something; as a son, I felt I should. Some final word - maybe just to say the word 'Father' or maybe just to say goodbye. But the words failed me. I turned on my heel and left the graveside without speaking to anyone, without looking back. It was sad that this man lived without us and died without us. Sadder still, he had lived without God and, as far as I know, died without God. I felt eternity had separated us, yet felt no sense of loss. [98]

He was buried in an unmarked grave that was soon

---

[98] Sadly I was never able to help him. His sudden death prevented me from doing so. He died, as far as I know, without being able to make his peace with God or man. Before he died he had spent many a night, so my brother told me, screaming in horror of the nightmares that plagued him. These were, no doubt, triggered off by the excuses he made and the things he had seen – and done.

levelled in a quest to prevent the graves of war criminals becoming a point of pilgrimage for equally deluded Nazi sympathisers who saw them as heroes. Today only I know the site of his burial. He left no trace. The only reminders of his existence are the yellowing pages of his trial in the archives of Germany and Austria.

The Company My Father Kept

Some people say that I judged my father too harshly, that he was a victim of his environment, that he had no choice but co-operate or starve. There is some truth in this, as the people of his generation have been hijacked by the force of National Socialism against which they had no defence. At the same time this does not negate the power of choice of the company you keep. John F. Kennedy said *"you are judged by the company you keep."* The company my father kept speaks as loud as the crimes he committed.

To piece together my father's social environment, we have to make some assumptions based upon the things we know. We know that he was a committed Nazi who disliked the Jews and an Austrian who served the Reich in a foreign country. This would automatically create an environment of a company of *Kameraden* who share the same *Heimatland* i.e. Austria, speak the same language, Austrian, and who hold to the same 'vision' in which the Jews are destined to perish.

They were all local men who lived in the relative small area of Upper Austria. In this respect it is not too difficult to piece together my father's social environment.

Besides his fellow deputies, the killers of Rabka[99], there is *Maximilian Grabner*. SS- Untersturmführer Grabner served in Katowice, a few miles north of Rabka. As Gestapo chief of Auschwitz he was responsible for the systematic torture of hundreds of people (see footnote 33).

---

[99] See Figure 19

Hermann Höfle was born in Salzburg on June 19, 1911. He joined the *NSDAP* on August 1, 1933, with party number 307,469. In 1937, he became *SS-Sturmbannführer of SS-unit 1/76*. Like my father, he trained at the officers' school in Dachau, after which he served in the *Selbstschutz* in Nowy Sacz in southern Poland, a few miles east of Rabka. He later participated in the genocide of Mogilew, Ukraine where 45,467 people were murdered by Einsatzgruppe B (see footnote 10).

Franz Stangl was, like my father, a musician who played the zither. Given this skill and the close proximity of Stangl's hometown of Wels, I have no doubt that these two men knew each other well. As commandant of Sobibor's and Treblinka death camps, he held the rank of *SS-Obersturmführer* - responsible for the death of almost a million people. (See footnote 62). Like my father, he was tracked down by Wiesenthal and arrested. Although imprisoned with my father, he managed to escape with the help of bishop Hudal's ODESSA ratline. He was re-arrested in 1967 and given a life sentence for genocide. (He and my father both died of heart failure within less than a year of each other.)

Johann and Wilhelm Mauer, two sadistic murderers who killed 12,000 people (see footnote 49) were members of the Einsatzgruppen in Rabka and soul buddies on their flight from Poland.

These are a few individuals of the company my father kept. (There will be many others we shall never know about). Their character reveals to me the kind of person my father was, in the words of Miguel de Cervantes who said in 1567, *"Tell me what company you keep and I will tell you what you are."*

Some of these men admitted the killings while saying *"my conscience is clear, I only did my duty"* (Stangl), *"I did it in the interest of my family"* (Grabner), *"I only followed orders"* (everybody else).

FIGURE 24

You are judged by the company you keep.[100]

---

[100] John F. Kennedy

Like it or not, I had to learn to accept the fact that my father must have been, like his friends, a characterless individual who had no fear of God and no qualms in murdering innocent civilians. The historian and moralist Lord Acton (1834–1902) coined the phrase *'power corrupts, absolute power corrupts absolutely'*. The evil of National Socialism consisted in giving power to godless individuals, thereby corrupting the normally good moral standard which resides in most human beings. It is said that you can chose your friends but you cannot chose your family. With this fact and with the information I uncovered, I had the privilege to make different decisions to the ones my ancestors made. But this did not mean that it was easy or automatic. My psychological heritage had formidable power that was corrupting me even after the death of my father.

I could have made excuses as many do, blaming my parents or my environment for my behaviour.

> *Don't let yourself be victimised by the age you live in. It is not the times that will bring us down, any more than its society…..there is a tendency today to absolve individuals of moral responsibility and treat them as victims of social circumstance. You buy that and you pay with your soul. …..what limits people is lack of character. (Tom Robbins)* [101]

I soon discovered that to live a different life I had to stop making the abuse my excuse. I had to face the issues and take responsibility for my behaviour and my lifestyle.

Battle against the Nazi Legacy

Though I was saved from the powers of demonic forces which had engulfed millions during the horrors of Nazi rule, I found it difficult to live out my Christian life. The absence

---

[101] Tom Robbins, Still Life with Woodpecker, No Exit press, London,2001, pp. 116

of a father role model and lack of family life contributed to my lack of character. I soon learned that new life in Christ meant a renewing and restoration of character for faith to function properly. Though I was truly born again, I needed to learn new behaviourism, acquire better attitudes, change the way I thought and spoke. Above all I needed to change the company I kept, as the saying goes:

Bad company corrupts good character.

This was a major threat to my new life and a certain cause for my downfall. But I was caught, like a fly in a spider's web, unable to free myself from the environment I had grown up in. The low life was my former environment, where I felt at home in the company of losers, thieves and criminals. With every new friendship I made I was unnoticeable drawn deeper into a life of crime, drugs and drink.

On top of that, the opposition from a semi-religious Nazi environment and the close proximity of criminal elements, made life for this young Christian very difficult. Accusations soon gave way to attacks, temptations and trials of all kinds that shook my faith. I began to waver and compromise. Some of my former criminal acquaintances tried to pin things on me; police questionings increased. I was beginning to falter. It seemed as if Satan tried to drag me back to the pit I escaped from.

The bad company I kept definitely had a corrupting effect on the reconstruction of my life. Because I had made slow progress as a Christian, the past was catching up fast. A drug dealer friend was on the run from those he had cheated. He wanted to break with his old life; they wanted to kill him.

I spent day and night watching over him while he was doing 'cold turkey', trying to break his drug habit. He was suicidal and delirious at the same time. For two weeks I managed to keep him safe, when he suddenly disappeared. He left some instructions of a major drug deal taking place in

Linz, which he wanted me to pass on to the police. I decided to use the opportunity to break with my evil environment by passing the information to the police.

A BULLET MEANT FOR ME

You may assassinate me, but you cannot intimidate me.[102]

Arriving home late one night, I was unaware that someone was waiting for me with a gun. I was about to open the door of our miserable abode when something exploded in the back of my head. Blind with pain I stumbled through the door and fell to the floor. Writhing in agony I held my head, blood pouring though my fingers. I could not think what had happened; the pain was too great for me to think. I barely managed to kick the door shut. When the throbbing

---

[102] Werner Oder

subsided enough for me to stumble to the bathroom, I discovered that I had been shot! Fortunately the bullet had just grazed my head. I had been lucky. As soon as I had recovered, instead of making good the break from the lowlife, I decided on revenge. I had managed to find out who it was who had shot me. I was going to get even. For days I planned and plotted and eventually tracked him down to his scummy bedsit in the slums of our town.

I was out of my mind. The hereditary tendency of hatred and cold blooded murder had caught up with me again. I had to get out but was caught in the web. Knowing that God was my only hope, I prayed for deliverance.

Chapter 5

Don't rob yourself the joy of this season by wishing you were in a future or a past one. [103]

Schloss Klaus

God sent me help though wonderful people: *The Torchbearers*. As a branch of *Capernwray Missionary Fellowship*, founded by Army Major Ian Thomas, the Torchbearers restored an old castle in the Austrian mountains, Schloss Klaus. They used it for Christian work among young people

---

[103] Cheryl Biehl

of post-war Austria. Schloss Klaus became my lifeline and my help in times of trouble. When my faith began to waver they graciously took me in, loved me and prayed for me, teaching me God's ways. They were true friends and men of quality.

> *Associate yourself with men of good quality if you esteem your own reputation; for it is better to be alone than in bad company.*[104]

At the invitation of *Capernwray Missionary Fellowship*, I travelled to England to attend their Bible school. There the prevailing Christian atmosphere and the dynamic teaching at Capernwray made a deep impression upon my life. During the two years at Capernwray, God reformed my life and my character, changing me from who I was to whom I was supposed to be.

Mission Impossible

My father's death, some 3 years previously highlighted an ongoing struggle inside me. Though I was free from the satanic curse of Nazi Germany, I was still struggling with finding the right attitude toward my parents. I felt neglected and betrayed by them, yet I knew it was imperative for me to find a way to honour my parents. Seeing my struggles in this respect, Jack a close friend, explained to me the significance of the 5th commandment:

> *'Honour your father and mother' - which is the first commandment with a promise... that it may go well with you... that you may enjoy ...life on earth.*[105]

But no matter how hard I tried I could not, I was unable to honour them for all their crimes, their neglect, their lack of parenting. In fact, I despised them for their cowardice and

---

[104] George Washington
[105] Ephesians 6:2 NIV

their prejudice toward the Jews.

"Your parents were not your choice, they were God's," Jack said. *"In choosing your parents, God revealed His plan and destiny for you. Your question 'why' is the wrong question. There are seldom answers to the 'why' question. You need to ask 'how'. How am I going to fulfil God's command?"* Jack insisted. He was a minister and a friend of Friedrich Bonhoeffer, one of the few church men who spoke against the Nazis in Germany.

Gently but persistently Jack helped me understand that I needed to ask 'how' not 'why'. How was I to honour a man like my father whom I despised and hated? How was I to honour a mother I openly charged with neglect, whom I accused for being responsible for my lingering illnesses?

FIGURE 26

A good friend contributes more to your future than a thousand enemies to your misfortune.

I did not understand why God chose this kind of man as my father. I would have preferred to be born into a Christian family. Thinking about the things Jack said to me, I had to force myself to accept my parents as the choice God made. Clearly, I could not honour my father for his crimes. However I could honour him as God's chosen instrument through which He brought me into the world so that I could experience God's salvation and deliverance. God chose them to give me a testimony and make me a man through whom He could change the world.

Because of my psychological heritage I understood that it is only in God that we discover our origin, our identity, our meaning, our purpose, our significance and our destiny; all other paths lead to a dead end. In forgiving I had to go where I had not been before. Stepping onto the unknown territory of accepting my heritage, I had to see it as a God-given opportunity to blaze a trail through the thorny jungle of the past, to leave a path for others to find the way to freedom.

Do not go where the path may lead, go instead where there is no path and leave a trail.[106]

Through faith in Jesus Christ, I discovered God's amazing destiny for me: to go where no one else had been and leave a trail for others to find the way to life. I cannot claim any superior solution to the difficulties of life; I can only say that it is God who turned evil into something wonderful and good.

Professor Dan Bar-On asked: *How do the children of the perpetrators overcome the burden of their parent's guilt?*[107]

People find this a difficult concept: how can anyone overcome the guilt of others? Is it possible for me to overcome the guilt of my parents? I am often asked the

---

[106] Ralph Waldo Emmerson
[107] Dan Bar-On, Legacy of Silence, Havard University Press, New York, 1989,

question, *"Have you forgiven your father?"* Many say, *"How can you forgive such a person like your father? After all he has done, the blackest hell is reserved for him."*

Unforgiveness is often used as a punishment in the mind of a victim toward the oppressors. However, unforgiveness does not hurt the oppressor. It only hurts the victim who keeps the pain alive through inability to release it. I often asked Holocaust survivors, *"Have you not suffered long enough? Have you not endured enough pain? Would you not like to be rid of that pain in your soul that makes you a prisoner of the past?"*

Forgiveness is neither easy, nor cheap. It is not found in the human soul, nor can it be conjured up in the mind of well-meaning men. Essentially, forgiveness is not a human attribute in that it does not grow naturally in the human heart. True forgiveness is an act of God, a gift if you like, which He freely gives to those who ask. Through this Divine gift, God supernaturally touches our will (so we are willing to forgive), our spirit (to give us the strength to do it), our heart (forgiveness that does not come from the heart is hypocritical) and our soul (to deal with the emotional/psychological aspects of forgiveness).

Forgiveness is more than saying sorry. True forgiveness deals with resentment, anger and deep seated pain in the soul of those wronged. Jesus defined it in his prayer on the cross:

Father forgive them for they know not what they are doing.[108]

During a great inner conflict, I grasped the fact that I could not forgive my father for what he had done to others. Only God could do this, and I was not God. I could only forgive him for what he had done to me.

I took the only photograph of my father in my hand and thanked God for the life he gave me through this man. I then asked God to forgive him for all the evil he did do and the good he did not do. With deep inner struggle I forgave this

---

[108] Luke 23:34 NIV

man for the father he never was. I did this to the best of my ability, willing it to be so, wanting it to be eternally true.

For the first time in my life I then discovered a pity for the man I called father. I did not hate him any longer but saw him as a poor deluded individual whose life choices robbed him of all the hopes and joys that could have been his. Worst of all, it robbed him of his eternal destiny.

When I arose from my knees, the internal cloud of bitterness, which had darkened my soul, lifted. Instead of hatred I experienced an inexplicable love filling the previous dark hole inside me.

To Forget is Impossible

The cruel attitude of an ignorant world says *"oh, forget it and move on."* But how can you *move on* if you are unable to forget it? Can one ever forget? Is it ever possible to overcome the horrors of the past by *forgetting* them?

I do not think it is humanly possible to forgive and forget. I have the greatest of sympathy with Holocaust survivors, many of them dear friends, who emphatically say, *"We can never forgive and we will never forget."*

There are things that are impossible to forget. I will never forget the nightmares. The Holocaust is a nightmare impossible to forget and I for one will make sure that the world will not forget one of the greatest tragedies in human history - one that God will never forget.

I was reminded of this during a trip to Switzerland in Spring 2010, when the Icelandic Volcano Eyjafjallajokull erupted, sending a huge ash cloud over Europe, paralysing all air travel. No planes flew, the trains were overbooked, no buses and coaches could cope with six million travellers grounded worldwide by the ash fallout. While I was praying for a way to get home, an American woman prayed for the Lord to show her why this was happening. She was stuck in Israel, while I was stuck in Switzerland. The Lord showed her that the combination of the ash cloud and the six million travellers were a sign that He had not forgotten the six million people turned to ash in the death camps of Europe.

To forget is impossible. The indelible memories and graphic images of the past are inerasably etched on the memory bank of our mind. There old and painful feelings are stored, triggering off negative emotions that bring the past to life. When this takes place, the past becomes a monster that will try to swallow up the future. We must make peace with our past so it won't mess up our future.

While it is impossible to forget, we must find a way to lay the past to rest. This was as relevant for me as it is for Holocaust survivors today, though my 'psychological Holocaust' as the son of a Nazi is nothing compared with the real Holocaust Jewish survivors had to endure. Nonetheless I had to come to the conclusion that nothing that is done today can undo the past. No repentance, reconciliation, remorse or regret can bring six million people back from the dead. Though we cannot change the past, we can determine our future - despite the past.

There is a past which is gone forever, but there is a future which is still our own.[109]

Rabbi Sha-ul from Tarsus explains to us that forgetting is not acting as if it never happened, but that there is a forgetting that enables us to move into the future:

But one thing I do: Forgetting what is behind and straining towards what is ahead, I press on towards the goal to win the prize for which God has called me heavenwards in Christ Jesus.[110]

There is a way of dealing with traumatic memories. There is freedom from the torment of the past, through the right kind of forgetting. Forgetting does not mean losing

109 F.W.Robertson
110 Philippians 3:13 NIV

awareness of past events. That would be amnesia. It means releasing the pain of the memory, like you remove the poison from a snake bite. When I placed my trust in the Lord Jesus Christ whom I believe to be the Jewish Messiah, He delivered me from the demons of Nazi Germany and removed the pain of the past that was threatening my future.

The thing I like to remember best is the future.

Holocaust in the Human Heart ?

Former Israeli President Shimon Peres, speaking at the German Bundestag on January 27, 2010, opened his address by reciting the Kaddish in memory of six million Jews who were murdered by the Nazis. He continued by saying:

On January 27, 1945, the world awoke to the fact, somewhat too late, that six million Jews were no longer among the living. The Holocaust raises painful questions that touch on the infinite depth of a man's soul. To which depth can the evil in man sink? And to what extent can a people that knew culture and respect intellect, remain silent? What kind of atrocities can be performed? How much can a moral compass be silenced? How can a nation consider itself to be a superior race and others inferior? [111]

As the son of a Nazi war criminal, I have agonised over this question many times. How can a people - how could my people - who were lovers of classical music, who enjoyed the pinnacle of a culture, who attend the great religious oratorios of Mozart, Handel and Bach, embark upon a killing spree of such unspeakable proportions?

What was it that caused decent men and women who had lived a relatively peaceful existence to turn almost overnight into monsters? Many people have tried to find answers as to how a civilized people can turn overnight into

---

[111] www.bundestag.de

monsters. Some say that these historical horrors were caused by a clash of culture. This is one issue that is often brushed under the carpet, especially in Austria. The people of Austria are proud of their culture, their musicians and poets. As Europeans they have considered themselves on the pinnacle of civilisation. So did the Englishman Cecil Rhodes who said in 1877:

> *I contend that we are the first race in the world; it is better for the human race the more of the world we populate. God has obviously chosen the English speaking race to be his tool through which he will bring about justice, freedom and peace in this world. If there is a God I think he would like me to ... expand the influence of the English speaking race.* [112]

This kind on nationalism has become the scourge of history. The British convinced themselves that they were a superior race. So did the Nazis, who used nationalism as an excuse to kill inferior races. Irish nationalism resulted in decades of terrorism. Nationalism in Rwanda sparked of genocide etc. Political nationalism is totally in opposition to God's nationalism. God's nationalism is based upon His Grace, through which He chooses the nations for His purpose.

Cecil Rhodes has by now found out that there was a God, and He was neither English nor German. In fact He revealed Himself as the God of Israel, who chose the Jews and not the Brits, Germans or Austrians to be His chosen people. It is through the Jews that culture came to Europe. The day we killed the Jew, Europe died. The Spanish writer Sebastian Vilar Rodrigez wrote on January 5, 2008:

> *I walked down the street in Barcelona, and suddenly discovered a terrible truth - Europe died in Auschwitz. We killed six million Jews and replaced them with 20 million Muslims. In Auschwitz we burned a culture, thought,*

---

[112] http://en.wikipedia.org/wiki/Cecil_Rhodes

creativity, talent. We destroyed the chosen people, truly chosen, because they produced great and wonderful people who changed the world. [113]

Austro-Germanic Death Cult

The English-speaking world generally assumes that all German-speaking people are the same. Nothing can be further from the truth. Germans and Austrians are as different as the English and the Americans. Unlike the Germans, Austrians are less regimented and less clinical. Their general way of life is laid-back and easy-going: in one word, 'gemütlich'[114]. They are a friendly folk who love their culture, their beer and their songs.

Adapted over the centuries, their cuisine is unsurpassed, their coffee houses famous, their skiing ability legendary. The well-known Austrian 'Gemütlichkeit' is made up of a mixture of romanticism, melancholy and love for harmonious music. Heavy rock music and McDonald's fast food are having a hard time in Austria.

Yet behind the thin masquerade of easygoing and light-hearted Austrian 'Gemütlichkeit' lies a chaotic mass of dark barbaric forces and morbidity, possibly inspired by the misfortunes of the old Austro-Hungarian Empire. This, together with a tribal dislike of foreigners, a hatred of non-white races and a sickly sense of Austrian sentimentality created a kind of nationalism that was to defend its emotional territory to the death. In addition to this, their earthy obsession with the Vaterland, emotional songs about *Die Heimat* (the homeland) and the mutual comfort of the beer evolved gradually into a religion for the initiated. The beer halls became the cathedrals to their schemes, Adolf Hitler their 'Saviour', the Aryans the chosen race, and Hitler's book

---

[113] Quoted in: www.faithfreedom.org/.../all-european-life-died-in-auschwitz-by-sebastian- vilar-rodrigez/

[114] See glossary

Mein Kampf their Bible.

Another reason could be the deep-seated natural superstition of the Austrians. Though traditionally catholic, many Austrians happily adhere to superstitious practises alongside their religion. Hitler was very superstitious.

His 'witchdoctor' Dr. Friedrich Krohn designed the Nazi flag with the Swastika, known to devil worshippers as the fylfot cross. The fylfot cross represent the hammer of the pagan god Thor who crushes the skulls of his enemies with deadly effect.

In ancient occult myths the swastika represents the broken arms of the Cross of Jesus Christ as a symbol of satan's victory over Jesus. Thus the satanic German/Austrian coalition became the pioneer of 20th century paganism; in the words of Hitler:

> *Neither Catholic nor Protestant has any future left. At least not for the Germans. Nothing will stop me stamping our Christianity in Germany, root and branch. One is either a Christian or a German, you cannot be both ... The clergy will be made to dig their own graves. They will betray their God to us...*[115]

It was of this the German Jew Heinrich Heine warned in his 18th century poem. Born in Düsseldorf to Jewish parents, Heine's prophetic writings were banned during the Nazi era. He prophesied a century before Nazi Germany:

> *Christianity has occasionally calmed the brutal German lust for battle, but cannot destroy that savage joy. And when once that restraining talisman, the cross is broken, the old stone gods will rise from unremembered ruins and Thor will leap to life again and bring down its gigantic hammer upon the Gothic cathedrals.*[116]

100 years later his words came true as Hitler's brutal

---

[115] www.123helpme.com/view.asp?id=149044
[116] Heine H., Religion and Philosophy in Germany (1832)

horde waved the swastika in their battle against the *restraining force of the cross of Jesus Christ,* bringing down the demonic hammer of Thor on the Gothic Cathedrals of the Christians and the Synagogues of the Jews.

The War Within

The main reason for the Holocaust, however, lies in the human heart - in every human heart. The prophet Jeremiah states, *"The heart is deceitful above all things, and desperately wicked: who can know it?"* [117] The NT gospel writer Mark penned a commentary on Jeremiah's revelation:

> *What comes out of a man is what makes him 'unclean'. For from within, out of men's hearts, come evil thoughts, sexual immorality, theft, murder, adultery, greed, malice, deceit, lewdness, envy, slander, arrogance and folly. All these evils come from inside and make a man 'impure'.* [118]

The problems in this world are not economic or political as the politicians would like us to believe. They are not caused by governments or dictators. They are caused by the very things that are deeply lodged in every human heart. The Holocaust happened because the seeds of the Holocaust resided in the human heart. It started with evil thoughts, such as *'the Jews are Untermenschen'* (the Jews are sub-human). If you think this long enough, you start believing it. Once you believe it, you say it. *'What comes out of a man makes him unclean and impure',* sinful. When others hear you say it, they start to think about it and eventually start believing it. Once you believe in something, you begin to act it out. Since evil thoughts reside next to 'murder' in the human heart, human beings want to murder those they 'think' are evil.

W.A.Tozer said, [119] *"Sow a thought, reap an act. Sow an act,*

---

[117] Jeremiah 17:9 KJV
[118] St.Mark 7:20-23 NIV
[119] W.A.Tozer, The Pursuit of God, Authentic Lifestyle (Dec 1987),

reap a habit. Sow a habit reap a character; sow a character, reap a destiny."

Like it or not, every human being is capable of participating in a Holocaust. That is why the world has gone from Auschwitz to Vietnam to Korea to Rwanda to Sudan to Bosnia to Iraq and Afghanistan in a few short decades. It is not the nations which are the problem; it is the human heart of every member of society. That is why we cannot change a society by improving their economy or securing their borders. Nor can we improve the quality of life by creating more laws or building bigger prisons. The only way to change society is to change the heart of the individual.

I have often been asked, *"Given the love you have for Israel, why did you convert to Christianity and not to Judaism?"* The answer is simply this: because of the wickedness of my heart I was unable to keep one of the Ten Commandments, let alone the other nine. It would have been impossible for me to even attempt to keep the 613 laws of Judaism. Even if I could, it still would not deal with the deep seated 'impurity' of my heart. It is a strange paradox that there are people who claim to keep all 613 laws of Judaism and still hate their neighbours.

The reason why I became a Christian was because I somehow knew that God was the only one who had the power to change my heart. The prophet Ezekiel recorded the wonderful promise in answer to Jeremiah's dilemma of the heart of man:

> *I will give you a new heart and put a new spirit in you; I will remove from you your heart of stone and give you a heart of flesh. And I will put my Spirit in you and move you to follow my decrees and be careful to keep my laws.*[120]

The Bible does not talk about a heart transplant here.

---

[120] Ezekiel 36:26 NIV

King David prayed, *"Create in me a pure heart."* [121] It talks about a new creation, where the Creator of the human heart reaches deep into our soul and removes the things that make a man impure. Ezekiel records the process of this re-creation:

> *I will sprinkle clean water on you, and you will be clean; I will cleanse you from all your impurities.* [122]

God's new creation of the human heart is a wonderful process, although not always very pleasant. Bit by bit, as we yield our hearts to Him, He removes our inner evils which are the cause of all conflicts and wars in this world,

> *What causes wars, and what causes fightings among you? Is it not your passions that are at war within you?* [123]

The cause of international conflict starts within the human heart. When we give God our hearts, He removes *evil thoughts* and replaces them with good thoughts. His forgiveness cleanses and delivers us of our internal wars and replaces these with holiness, Joy and Peace.

> *My son, give me your heart*
> *and let your eyes keep to my ways.* [124]

True Christianity has nothing to do with Christian 'religion'. Religion has to do with trying to keep laws and regulations. These are unable to change the human heart, as our overflowing prisons tell us. One can be religious, like the Catholic priest Josef Tiso, and still have a desperately wicked heart which consented to the murder of Jews in the name of his imaginary god.

Alois Hudal may have been the priest in charge of the Church of *Santa Maria del' Anima,* yet still had a heart full of deceit which helped war criminals escape from 'their

---

[121] Psalm 51:10 NIV
[122] Ezekiel 26:25 NIV
[123] James 4:1 KJV
[124] Proverbs 23:26 NIV

tormentors'.

Martin Luther may have been a great religious reformer. Yet deep in his heart he harboured resentment, even hatred, of the very people who wrote the book that inspired him to declare *sola scriptura*, that the Bible is the inspired Word of God. These are some of the reasons why Jews deeply resent Christianity, as for hundreds of years they had suffered at the hands of those who called themselves followers of Jesus Christ. For that very same reason, many Christian Churches teach replacement theology and take the lead in boycotting Israel. They are quick to side with anyone who finds fault with Israel without lifting a finger to help her in times of need. Religion, without the power of the Holy Spirit at work in the heart of man, is deadly.

The heart of man, every man, is desperately wicked; only God can change man's heart. Laws and regulations could not change my heart. It required the power of the Spirit of God to *'change my sorrow into joy and give me the garment of praise instead of the spirit of heaviness, despair and depression.'* [125]

> *If we walk in the light, as he is in the light, we have fellowship with one another, and the blood of Jesus, his Son, purifies us from all sin. If we claim to be without sin, we deceive ourselves and the truth is not in us. If we confess our sins, he is faithful and just and will forgive us our sins and purify us from all unrighteousness.* [126]

What the world needs is what every member of the Christian Church needs - a change of heart.

> *The Spirit of the LORD came upon (Saul) in power, and he was changed into a different person.* [127]

When man's heart is changed by the Power of *Ruach*

---

[125] Isaiah 61:1-3 NIV
[126] 1.John 1:7-9 NIV
[127] 1 Samuel 10:6 NIV

HaKodesh [128], the individual becomes what God destined him to be. When man's heart is changed, the world changes.

> *Be who God meant you to be and you will set the world on fire.* [129]

---

[128] See glossary

[129] St.Catherine of Siena, 25 March 1347 in Siena – 29 April 1380

Chapter 6

FIGURE 27

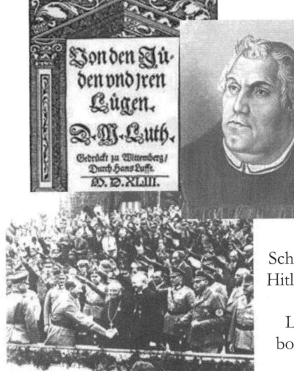

Austrian Abbot Schachleitner welcomes Hitler as enthusiastically as Hitler welcomed Luther's Anti-Semitic book *Von den Juden und ihren Lügen*.

Men never do evil so completely and cheerfully as when they do it from a religious conviction.[130]

The Death Wish of Christian Religion

On September 15, 1909, 56 leading Clergy of the Evangelical Alliance of Germany met to discuss reports of a great phenomenon which was occurring in America, Wales and other parts of the world. These reports spoke of a great spiritual awakening among the population in Azusa Street of Los Angeles, where many people had turned to God because

---

[130] Blaise Pascal, French mathematician, Physicist, 1623 – 1662

of a special work of the Holy Spirit. Supernatural healings took place and many prophecies were given by ordinary people who were impacted by God. In Wales, pictures of Christ appeared on the walls of Churches supernaturally, which many devoted individuals believed to be a warning from God of a great suffering to come upon the world.

The Confusion of the Church in Germany

The German clergymen discussed for 19 hours the present outpouring of the Holy Spirit and the consequential birth of what is known to day the Pentecostal movement. They concluded that this was not from God but from the devil and stated:

> *The so called Pentecostal Movement is not from above but from below ... Demons are at work in it, led with cunning by Satan, lies are mixed together with truth to lead the Children of God astray ... Neither the personal faithfulness and devotion of some individuals, nor the healings, tongues and prophecy etc. which accompany this movement can change our conviction that this movement is from below...*

They effectively said, *"We do not want another Pentecost."* This declaration led to a national rejection of the Holy Spirit that is affecting Germany to this day. Because the German Christians did not acknowledge the Holy Spirit, they were later unable to identify the spirit from hell which brought Hitler on the scene. The theological prejudice of the German church opened the door to the demons of anti-Semitism who came in and smashed the gothic cathedrals, burned the synagogues and destroyed the Jews.

The Compromise of the Church in Austria

The great majority of Austrians welcomed Hitler, supported his cause and believed in his ideals, despite their religion. How can religious people be so deluded?

One week after Austria joyfully welcomed 'Adi' [131] home, Austrian bishops blessed the national socialism on Adolf Eichmann's birthday, the March 18, 1938, stating:

From Inner conviction and with free will we, the undersigned bishops of the Austrian Church province, acknowledge joyfully that the national socialist movement ... has contributed greatly toward the growth of social politic for the German Reich...[132]

Within days of the church blessing the Nazis, prisoners from the concentration camp in Dachau were transferred to Linz to start the construction of Mauthausen concentration camp on August 7, 1938.

The Austrian church simply failed to recognise the spirit from hell that was rising in their midst. Where did this religious deception which drew scores of devout Catholics and Lutherans into the web of satanic conspiracy against humanity come from? The answer lies with many so-called church fathers whose theology was used to form the base of the modern church. One of them was Martin Luther.

The Contradiction in the Faith of Martin Luther

To give him his due, as professor of the Wittenberg Theological Institute in Germany, Luther changed the world through his revolutionary statement *'sola fide, sola gratia, sola Scriptura'*. The consequences of this re-discovery have resulted in millions of believers discovering that salvation is by *faith alone, through Grace alone, by the Scriptures alone*. They, like myself, are indirectly indebted to Luther for his rediscovery that salvation and eternal life can only be

---

[131] Nickname given by Hitler's Austrian followers
[132] Exhibit by the Federal Ministry of Interior, 1938 Nazi Rule in Austria, Austrian Documentation Centre of the Resitance Movement, 1998, pp. 15 (Translated from German and abbreviated by the author)

received as a gift of Grace through faith, according to the Bible and not through human effort, religiosity or good works like giving to charity. In teaching this, Luther upheld the unchangeable reality that one cannot enter heaven through the vague superstition of self-righteousness and good deeds.

Though Luther excelled in one doctrine, he failed in another. His achievements may have been proudly emphasised by the stalwarts of reformation, yet his failure to identify God in the New Testament as the God of Israel became a point of embarrassment to his denomination. Worse still, it led to religious anti-Semitism.

In his pamphlet *Von den Juden und ihren Lügen* ('the Jews and their lies'), Luther's anti-Jewish ranting turned the Reformation into a vehicle that carried the anti-Semitic spirit into all parts of its empire. This is a short excerpt of what the great reformer wrote in 1548:

> *What shall we Christians do with this damned, rejected race of the Jews? Since they live among us, and we know about their lying and blasphemy and cursing, we cannot tolerate them if we do not wish to share their lies, curses and blasphemy ... we must prayerfully and reverentially practise merciful severity.* [133]

Luther was not alone. There were other church men who held on to this lie: scholars, church fathers and theologians, passing on to their students the idea that God had finished with the Jews through the ancient heresy of replacement theology. Since the Church spoke out against the Jews in such a way, the Nazis later believed that in fulfilling Luther's mandate they were doing the will of God. Four hundred years later, it was printed in the Nazi newspaper *Der Stürmer*.[134] Editor Julius Streicher, who was later convicted

---

[133] en.wikipedia.org/wiki/On_the_Jews_and_Their_Lies
[134] Noble, Graham. "Martin Luther and German anti-Semitism," History Review (2002) No. 42:1-2.

and executed for inciting Germans to kill Jews, described it as the most radically anti-Semitic tract ever published. Is it any wonder that Lutherans like Eichmann actually believed they were doing the will of God in their persecution of the Jews?

Being blinkered by the heretic ideas of its forefather Martin Luther, the established Church of Germany and Austria largely failed to uphold the mandates of the very book they consider as being inerrant:

> *Rescue those being led away to death; hold back those staggering towards slaughter. If you say, "But we knew nothing about this," does not he who weighs the heart perceive it? Does not he who guards your life know it? Will he not repay each person according to what he has done?* [135]

This ancient prophecy reads like a sad commentary of Austrian and German attitudes where people still claim today, *"we knew nothing about this."* Simon Wiesenthal reflects on this:

> *The schools would fail through their silence, the Church through its forgiveness,[136] and the home through the denial and silence of the parents. The new generation has to hear what the older generation refuses to tell it.[137]*

The silence[138] and compromise of the Church during the Nazi regime is one regrettable chapter in history many would want to wish away. But no matter how much denial is taking place in this respect, this indelible blot on the pages of church history will neither fade nor can it be erased.

---

135 The Bible: Proverbs 24:11-12 NIV

136 Wiesenthal does not criticise the principles of forgiveness here, but the easy forgiveness the Church offered to criminals who want absolution without repentance and forgiveness without remorse.

137 www.wiesenthal.com › ... › About › About Simon Wiesenthal (Introduction to The Sunflower)

138 Thankfully not all have failed and not all kept quiet. There were many who stood up and spoke at the peril of their lives, such as Dietrich Bonhoeffer. Indeed many preferred to share their fate with the people they tried to protect than remain silent. These are the true heroes of history. While many commemorate Holocaust memorial days, all too many forget the ongoing Holocausts of Christians in Arab countries.

It is interesting that the church's reason for adopting replacement theology is nothing less than ancient bigotry.

A narrow and bigoted replacement theology ... (is) just a liberal 'theology of denial' ... a means of distancing oneself from Israel.[139]

The thought behind this idea is, because Israel was so sinful God cut Israel off and replaced her with the Church.

It is interesting to note though, that what we call 'church' today seems to be more sinful than Israel ever was. So, if God replaced Israel because of her sin, then God must do the same to the church. This seems to be happening as we speak, especially in the Western world, where the church is being replaced by Islam.

This replacement is certainly financed by the oil of the Arab world who for decades have endeavoured to buy the favour of Western politicians. To good effect, as these are now bent on outlawing Christianity.

Anyone who hates the Jews also hates Jesus Christ.[140]

Once they get rid of the Christians and their 'mistaken zeal for Israel', the next step is to get rid of Israel itself. Western politicians want to build a world without Israel.

The demonic spirit that inspires radical fundamentalist Islam is the same spirit that has tried to destroy the Jewish people throughout history.[141]

But this will never happen. Whether or not politicians believe in God or not does not alter the fact that God IS. He is the God of Israel, who neither slumbers nor sleeps. Since

---

[139] Ulf Eckman Beloved/Hated Israel, Ulf Ekman Ministries, 2004, p. 121
[140] David Ben-Gurion, Nahaman Tamid, "Sholem Asch in the Eye of the Storm," Maariv, April 21, 1989.
[141] Howard Morgan, Lessons from the Olive tree, Howard Morgan ministries, © 2001, pp. 113

God never changes, He never changed his name, nor has he changed his mind over Israel. He has neither cut off the Jews nor has he finished with Israel:

> *God did not reject his people whom he foreknew ... for they will be grafted in ... and all Israel will be saved ... this is my covenant with them when I will take away their sin.*[142]

The phenomenon of anti-Semitism was and is only possible through the dulled conscience of the church. But the church needs to remember that you cannot worship Jesus Christ and hate his people; in hating the Jews you hate him who was born and bred a Jew.

Dörte von Westhagen in her book *Die Kinder der Täter* [143] calls the dulled conscience *'Der Massenschlaf des Gewissens'* ('the sleeping conscience of the masses'). The sleeping conscience seems to be the condition of the Western Church which is slumbering in her cozy world of make-believe: *"It won't come here, it won't affect me and, at any rate, Jesus is coming back soon when we will be raptured and taken out of our trouble."*

It is time for Christians to wake up to the reality that we have a mandate to *endure to the end*, not find a religious escape route. For Zion's sake we cannot and must not be silent at this time. The silence of my ancestors, with which they tried to cover the heinous crimes committed by the Nazis, made them as guilty as those who pulled the trigger.

> *The violence of the few is not as dangerous as the silence of many.*[144]

For Zion's sake and for the sake of my family's freedom, I felt that I had to break the conspiracy of silence. As Zionists we must do the same in the pews of the Christian establishment. It is time for the church to wake up out of her

---

[142] Romans 11:2-27 NIV
[143] Dörte von Westhagen, Die Kinder der Täter, Deutscher Taschenbuch Verlag, GmbH, München, 1987, pp.174
[144] Ken Burnett in a comment to this author

self-induced coma and realise her opportunity. I am convinced God is giving the church another chance.

> *Wake up, strengthen what remains and is about to die. But if you do not wake up, I will come as a thief.* [145]

---

[145] Rev.3:2-3 NIV

Chapter 7

The purpose of our existence as Christians is neither a ticket for a joy ride to heaven, nor an insurance policy to escape hell.[146]

The church is Christ's body, represented by the local church. Indeed God's purpose is for every Christian to belong to a local Church, not just to learn new things but to learn to serve the Lord, to become strong in order to make known God's Word and Will to the nations and their rulers:

His intent was that now, through the church, the manifold wisdom of God should be made known to the rulers and authorities in the heavenly realms, according to his eternal purpose which he accomplished in Christ Jesus our Lord.[147]

God wants the church of today to succeed where the church of 1938 has failed. For that reason God set me free, so that my life can be a vocal and visible testimony to the life-changing power of God.

The Blessing

Today I am free from the satanic legacy of terror and fear: no longer tormented by my father's past, no longer burdened by collective guilt, no longer troubled by the conspiracy of silence. I enjoy the immense freedom Christ brought to my soul. I am grateful to know God's peace and enjoying a wonderful life that has been blessed with total deliverance from the demonic heritage of Nazi Germany. In addition to this, my quest for the truth led me to discover my real identity and in doing so discover the purpose for my existence.

---

[146] Reinhard Bonnke during his speech to leaders, Fire Conference, Birmingham 1994
[147] Ephesians 3:10 NIV

If the Son shall set you free you shall be free indeed.[148]

God somehow turned the traumas of the past into something good. In line with his promise *'perfect Love casts out all fear'* [149], He made me fearless in the face of evil, giving me the courage of living the Christian life in a world that is once again turning to the dark principles of racism and anti-Semitism.

This freedom from the past and the courage for the future has not come as a result of some system of self-improvement or clever psychological trick. The freedom I am enjoying is solely due to the gracious work of God, who worked in my life powerfully, enabling me to overcome an evil legacy that has destroyed the lives of many. In line with the promise, He created in me a new heart. This process is challenging and still ongoing.

Without God, it is impossible to deal with such issues. When speaking about God I am not speaking about Him glibly. Neither am I talking about a vague concept in the sky, the 'something up there'. I am talking about the God and Father of our Lord Jesus Christ, who created the world and us in His image. He knows us better than we know ourselves and loves us with unending Love. He is the God of Israel, known to the Jews as the God of Abraham, Isaac and Jacob, who sent His Son to become the Messiah and Saviour of the world.

If Jesus Christ is not the Jewish Messiah, he cannot be the Saviour of the world.

Men are free to reject Him, as did my father, at the peril of their lives. *But those who have received Him and have believed in His name, He gave the power to become children of God.'*[150]

I now know the answer to 'who I am, why I was born and what the purpose of my existence on this troubled planet

---

[148] St. John 8:36 NIV
[149] 1.John 4:18 NIV
[150] Gospel of St.John 1:12 NIV

is'. I am immensely grateful to the God of all gods who, in His wisdom and through His great love, worked everything for my good and the good of others. God gave me those parents so that He could show me His deliverance. He allowed me to experience the horrors of hell and the evil of anti-Semitism so that He could show me His salvation. By His Spirit He changed my heart so I could have the power to change my world. He broke the bondage of the past to give me a wonderful destiny:

> *Consider then thyself and the nobility within thee, for thou art honoured above all creatures, in that thou art an image of God; thou art destined for greatness.*[151]

This is not just for people with great testimonies; this is for everybody who believes. If you believe, *you* are destined for greatness.

The Sign

In 1995 Time Magazine stated that the power of Adolf Hitler *'to obsess our century has remained undiminished'* and that Hitler was *'a spectre that continues to haunt the world.'*[152] When I read this statement I was reminded of a passage in the Bible where David, in righteous indignation, refused to accept the status quo in Israel:

> *What will a man get for killing this Philistine and putting an end to this abuse of Israel?*[153]

I began asking the Lord to show me what I could do to put an end to the international abuse of Israel. Apart from teaching the Western Church concerning the heresy of Replacement Theology, I wondered what else I could do. After praying a long time I saw the world *Poland* flash across

---

[151] Eckhart von Hochheim (1260-1327)
[152] Time Magazine May 8, 1995
[153] 1.Sam.17:26 NLT

my mind.

At the same time I felt I should visit the Polish village of Rabka where my father was caught up in unspeakable horrors against the Jewish people. I wanted to pray for forgiveness in the very place and say Kaddish for little Samuel Rosenbaum, praying for the remaining members of my family to be delivered from the curse. But I needed to be sure it was the right thing to do. I have seen too many people act on visions and dreams which were little more than vain imaginations. I asked the Lord for a sign. I did not have to wait long.

While scanning the war crime trial documents of 1948, my eyes fell on a particular name of an eye witness from the village of Rabka, who testified in court against my father's crimes. Out of pure curiosity I entered a computer search in order to find out what happened to her. To my utter amazement I learned that the witness and her brother, Marek, were still alive.

After tentative enquiries through Eric, a Jewish friend, I sent word that I would like to meet Marek. I assumed that if Marek was still alive he must be living in the US or in Israel. I had no idea where he was. Minutes after speaking to Eric, I returned home when the phone rang. A voice with a Polish accent asked what my name was. Confirming my name to the mysterious caller (something I do not generally do) there was a long pause until the voice said, *"Who was your father?"*

By that time I knew something unusual was happening. I mentioned the name of my father. After another long pause the voice said, *"I think I know who your father was."* It was Marek. During the little, somewhat pensive conversation I asked whether we could meet, being fully prepared to fly to The States to meet the man. He agreed and said that he would come to my house. *"When?"* I asked. *"Tomorrow afternoon,"* he said. *"I only live five minutes from you."* My mind flipped. All the years I spent on this investigation, the man who escaped from my father's death squad was actually living five minutes from me. The sign from God.

We arranged to meet the following day. I wondered how that meeting was going to go. Me, the son of the Nazi who contributed to the murder of Marek's family and Marek who survived my father's attempt to kill him.

Meetings like this are never easy; after all, face to face encounters of this kind are rare. Emotions run deep. Though not directly responsible, I felt responsible. I have met many survivors; it is always difficult. Some say, *"It's not your fault"*; others hate you for something you did not do. Who can blame them? What would my attitude be when confronted with the killers of my family? Would I be able to forgive, or turn into an avenger who wants blood?

If Marek ever found it hard to meet an Austrian descendant of those who oppressed his people, he rarely showed it. He was always polite and genuinely interested, but deep down inside I sensed a struggle and a hatred for my father, which I completely understood.

In seeing Marek carrying himself manfully as he speaks about his memories, I have nothing but admiration for a man who has survived the worst injustice in modern history. Over the years we have become friends. I got to know his wife and family; we love them and they love us. We have a very special relationship that is unique and difficult to comprehend. Marek and I meet regularly and often share our stories at speaking engagements.

God did not just send me a sign about Poland; He sent me a Polish Jew from the very place I wanted to visit. Having asked for one sign, God sent me two. After meeting another dear Jewish brother who regularly speaks at a conference in Auschwitz, I was invited to share in a very special reconciliation service at the death camp of Birkenau. As I walked through the camp I picked up some barb wire lying on the ground. Thinking about the service I was about to share I absentmindedly fashioned the barb wire into a cross.

Standing on the ramp of Auschwitz/Birkenau Concentration camp I thought about the million Jews who were murdered there under the leadership of the Austrian camp commander Rudolf Höss. As hundreds of people looked on, I lifted up the barb wire cross as a sign of God's love and forgiveness for one another. We stated that as long as we and our families shall live we would do all that it takes to prevent another Holocaust. While we were praying together people started pointing at the sky. Right above our heads a white cross appeared in the blue sky above – and every eye saw it.[154] To us this was God's way of saying *Amen*.

What are those signs about? Signs are said to follow those who believe. To me these signs became God's confirmations of the miracle of reconciliation between Jews and Gentiles through the Messiah, whose power can change the heart of the worst sinner. They are a reminder and confirmation to us that God has destined us for greatness, to be people who become world changers. To me these signs, significant as they are, are but a small pointer toward God's greater purpose to stand with Israel in a time where millions of exterminators are poised to finish what Hitler failed to do.

As Christians we are not a weak little bunch of fanatics. We are conquerors who are called to make history, overcomers through whom God changes the destiny of nations. There is no greater proof than Israel. When people like Herzl saw the Messiah[155] and acted upon his call to make a homeland for his people, he became a world changer and history maker who brought about the restoration of the land to its rightful owners. Yes, Israel is the rightful owner to the land.

---

[154] If you visit www.tucktonchristiancentre.co.uk you will be able to view this
[155] Herzl had a dream in which he met the Messiah, see Amon Elon Herzl, Holt Rhinehart & Whinston, Canada, 1975, pp.16

Israel belongs to the Jews — they fought for it under God's authority — they bought it under the British — they died for it in 1948! Let them live in peace while they wait for the coming of their Messiah! [156]

An Arab believer was asked by a Jewish journalist: *"whose land is it, yours or ours?"* The Arab Christian calmly replied,

I was born to hate Jews. I was taught from birth this land was ours and we should take it at any cost. Then Jesus Christ, the Jewish Messiah and Saviour of the world entered my heart. Since that time I no longer quibble over the rocks and sand of this land. I am but a pilgrim passing through on my way to a new home prepared for me beyond Jordan. This is not my land or yours, it is God's. [157]

I too was taught to hate the Jews, but when Jesus Christ, the Jewish Messiah, entered my heart he changed my world and turned the curse into blessing. Today I am blessed and walk in the blessings of Abraham which are detailed in Deuteronomy 28:1-14. Wherever I go I am blessed, in the country or the city. My wife is blessed and so is our marriage. We are greatly blessed with very beautiful children who are walking with the Lord, bringing up their children in the politically incorrect way of faith in the Messiah and love for Israel. We are walking under an open heaven, where God's Grace meets all our needs whatever they may be. He made me the head where I once was the tail. I am eternally grateful to the Lord who blessed me with heaven's unsearchable riches. Christ removed the curse that I may experience the blessings of God.

This knowledge I share with almost two billion Christians around the world. I have, like them, discovered my true identity in the purposes of the God of gods who sent

---

156 David Hathaway, Prophetic Vision, No 60/Summer 2011, pp. 7
157 Jamie Buckingham, A Way Through the Wilderness, Kingsway Publication, Eastbourne, 1984

His only Son to bring hope to this sad and dying world. In believing in Him, that is Jesus Christ, the Son of the living God, all men can be free and find forgiveness and life, experiencing the same joy and freedom from all evil. The experience of such change, from hatred to love, from anti-Semitism to Zionism is truly miraculous.

What do I do to support Israel and why do I love Israel? Not for the reasons Professor Dan Bar-On Ben Gurion University gives:

> *"Children of Nazis who became supporters of Israel did so out of guilt." He said that "they joined the victims and survivors and take the guilt of their forefather upon themselves as a way of making amends."* [158]

I cannot make amends, no matter how sorry I am for the Holocaust. I cannot undo the past and bring six million victims of Nazi atrocities back. I also cannot take my father's guilt upon me - it will not help the Jewish people. It would destroy me. What I can do is to love the Jews because the creator God declared:

> *For I am the LORD your God, who churns up the sea so that its waves roar - the LORD Almighty is his name. I have put my words in your mouth and covered you with the shadow of my hand - I who set the heavens in place, who laid the foundations of the earth, and who say to Zion, 'You are my people.'* [159]

I do this, because God put His Word in my mouth to *'Speak up for those who cannot speak for themselves.'* [160]

When He put His Word in my mouth, He also put the fire of His love in my heart for the people of this world, whatever their colour or their culture: for the Jews, for the Arabs, for all people who were created in God's image. This

---

[158] Dan Bar-On, The Legacy of silence, Harvard University, New York, 1989
[159] Isaiah 51:15-16 NIV
[160] Proverbs 321:8

includes Israel's enemies, members of Hamas, Hezbollah, the Palestinians, the people of Egypt and Assyria. In the light of the Love of God, Christ revealed, we must pray for our enemies. People do evil things because they do not know God. When we pray for our enemies, God will open their eyes to see His purpose for the nations.

The LORD Almighty will bless them, saying, "Blessed be Egypt my people, Assyria my handiwork, and Israel my inheritance. [161]

---

[161] Isa 19:25 NIV

The Lightning of God

It is hard to comprehend how the God of Israel had mercy on this child of a Nazi; how he opened my eyes to the mystery of Israel and the mystery of the Kingdom of God:

> *To you it has been granted to know the mysteries of the kingdom of heaven.*[162]

Fighting for survival as a Christian in an evil world, I had to learn that *'the kingdom of God is not a matter of talk but of power.'*[163] When God called me out of the darkness of a Nazi heritage into His wonderful light, *'I heard the voice of the LORD strike with flashes of lightning'.*[164] In His unfailing love He *'made his light shine into [my] heart to give me the light of the knowledge of the glory of God'.*[165] The light of His revelation unlocked the mystery of Israel for me, transforming my inner darkness into indescribable light. By His Grace I now live in the supernatural dimension of light. I am not unique in this. Every child of God is called to walk in this supernatural dimension where our prayers travel faster than the speed of light.

Walking in the heavenly light of God is the only way to reach our divine destiny. If we ever stop moving forward or walk in the twilight of human religion, the devils of the past, which travel at the speed of time, will catch up with us again.

---

[162] Matthew 13:11 NIV
[163] 1.Corinthians 4:20 NIV
[164] Psalm 29:7 NIV
[165] 2. Corinthians 4:6 NIV

For troubles without number surround me; my sins have overtaken me. (Psalm 40:12)

The lightning of God has kindled a fire in my bones that cannot be quenched. It has created in me a furnace of unshakable commission to bring light to the Christian church. Not just to stand with Israel and pray for the peace of Jerusalem, but to succeed where our Christian ancestors have failed in being a friend of Israel. To let our light shine requires more than just waving the Israeli flag while singing the Hatikvah. As we walk into the sunset of this world which is entering its closing stages, we need to display the nuclear power of Christ's resurrection. With Israel nearing Jacob's troubles and the world Armageddon, we need to live the resurrected life of those who were raised with Christ. When we walk in this indescribable light, our enemies will see the light of God's love and the Church will see Israel as the people and inheritance of God.

> *[God's] intent was that now, through the church, the manifold wisdom of God should be made known to the rulers and authorities in the heavenly realms, according to his eternal purpose which he accomplished in Christ Jesus our Lord.*[166]

---

[166] Ephesians 3:10 NIV

Epilogue

Our life is just a vapour, and time is short. We must redeem our time and make it count, for the days are evil. What is the point of gathering wealth, enjoy the luxuries of life and become rich and famous? Then you die.

Scores of war criminals who were never brought to justice died as wealthy men. Yet though they escaped human justice they never got away with anything, for every one of them will have to appear before God. We all have to. There will be a price to pay for the life we lived. We cannot afford to play 'trivial pursuit' with our lives. We will have to give an account to God about the life we lived. Our own personal goodness will not save us. Our good works will not save us. Our righteous acts, compared with those of God are *'like filthy rags.'*[167]

What we call good, God calls sin. For all sin there is hell to pay. Everyone has the privilege of choice, either pay for it themselves or accept the full payment Christ paid on the cross. He paid the price for all sin, He paid hell so that all who care to believe in Him can be forgiven and know the promise of Heaven.

When you believe in Jesus the Jewish Messiah, you will know the wonder of being saved from Satan's power and the stronghold of sin. My testimony in this book is a confirmation that God's saving power is real. No matter what you have done, no matter who you are, God wants to love you and be your friend.

If you call on the name of the Lord Jesus Christ and accept Him as your own personal Messiah and Lord, you will be saved from all sin and delivered from all evil:

And everyone who calls on the name of the LORD will be saved; for on Mount Zion and in Jerusalem there will be

---

[167] Isaiah 64:6 NIV

deliverance, as the LORD has said, among the survivors whom the LORD calls.[168]

God will turn your life around; He will bless you and make you successful in everything you do and set eternity into your heart. He will shine a ray of hope into your heart and kindle an eternal flame in you that will never go out. There are no losers in the Kingdom of God. With Christ in your life you will win.

You may want to pray these words now:

Heavenly Father, I confess that I have lived for myself and thereby sinned against You, against myself and the people around me. I ask for forgiveness of all sin and deliverance from all evil. I now accept Jesus as my Messiah and thank You that You sent Him to this world to pay the price for my sin. I now change my mind about living for myself and decide to live for You.

Cleanse me from all unrighteousness and deliver me from all evil. Fill me with Your Holy Power that I may know You and serve You to the end of my days. I pray this in the Name of Jesus the Messiah.

Amen.

---

[168] Joel 2:28 NIV

FIGURE 28

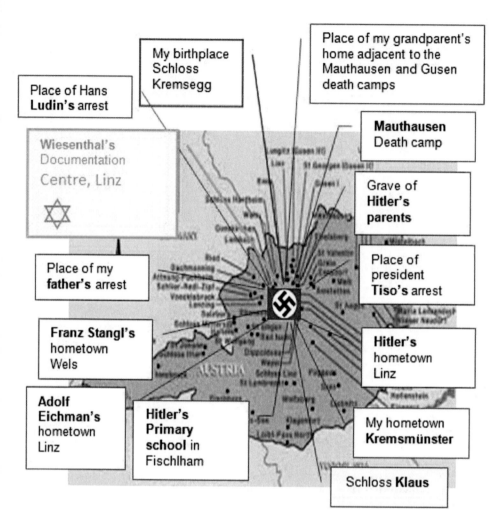

In this 100 square kilometre 'quadrangle of death' God created Life, healing and forgiveness.

Glossary

Angehörigen   members

Anschluss   Annex of Austria to Germany April 2, 1938

Das tausendjährige deutsche Reich the thousand year German Empire

Dokumentations Zentrum documentation centre

Einsatzgruppen   SS & SD death squads.

Führer   Leader

Gauleiter   The supreme territorial or regional Nazi Party authority

Gemütlich   cosy or comfortable

Gestapo   *Geheime Staatspolizei*, German: *secret state police*

GG   General Gouvernement, main part of occupied Poland made up of five districts (including Galicia).

GPK   Grenzpolizei – Kommissariat: A regional frontier HQ (border posts).

Heimatland   *home country*

Jetzt wird's aber Zeit German: *It's about time*

Judenrein   Nazi German euphemism for Semitic cleansing

Kameraden   comrades

Kapo   *Kamp Polizei*, German: *camp police*

KdS   German abbreviation: *Kommandeur der Sicherheitspolizei und des SD;* the KdS was the cadre responsible for mass executions and resettlement.

Kripo   *Kriminal Polizei*, German: *detective Police*

Kristall Nacht   Crystal night, November 9, 1938

NSDAP   National Socialist German Workers Party, or Nazi Party

Niemand darf erfahren wer ich bin nobody must discover who I am (or where I come from)

Reichsdeutsche   refers to German nationals living within the pre-1939 boundaries of the Third Reich.

Ruach HaKodesh Hebrew: *Holy Spirit*

Rückkehr unerwünscht Nazi German euphemism for return of prisoners not desired

SA: Sturmabteilung (Brown Shirts) Storm Troopers

Schupo   *Schutzpolizei.* Auxiliary police recruited in the eastern occupied territories from the local population.

Selbstschutz   self protection

Sipo-SD   Sicherheitspolizei – Sicherheitsdienst; German for Security Police and Security Service

SS-Schutzstaffel   (Lit. 'Defence echelon').

SS Ranks in this book

SS-Rottenführer	Corporal
SS-Unterscharführer	Sergeant
SS-Oberscharführer	Staff Sergeant
SS-Hauptscharführer	Sergeant-Major
SS-Sturmscharführer	Regimental Sergeant-Major
SS-Untersturmführer	2nd Lieutenant

Untersuchungshaft Detention while awaiting trial

Volksdeutsche   ethnic Germans, that is, people of German origin whose families had lived outside Germany for generations.

Waldviertel   northern part of Lower Austria

Wehrmacht   German for *Defence force*

Yeshuah HaMashiach Jesus the Messiah

Illustrations

Fig.

1. Author taking a break during investigation

2. 'Hütler' – Hitler's original family name. Grave stone of Zahnschirm, priest of Döllersheim

3. Primary school building Hitler attended in *Fishlham*, near Wels, Upper Austria. In 2000 a plaque was placed on the wall of the Old Schoolhouse with an embedded piece of granite taken from Mauthausen death camp.

4. Pressburg, now Bratislava castle with the Jewish *Zuckermandl* district where my grandparents lived

5. Mauthausen Death Camp

6. Mauthausen liberation – somewhere in the crowd of survivors are Simon Wiesenthal and Stefan Kuster

7. Wiesenthal, at first, was hunting the wrong man - businessman Hermann instead of his brother Wilhelm

8. The third man, (l to r) J.Tiso, H. Ludin and my father

9. Documents of father's NSDAP membership, admission of his arrest after the assassination of the Austrian Chancellor and the publicised death penalty upon all Nazis prior to the Anschluss in 1938. The Nazis defied the death penalty by sticking swastikas with the logo '*Trotz Verbot Nicht Tot*', (despite prohibition we are not dead).

10. Rare photograph of what appears to be my father with my two brothers Wilhelm and Peter paying tribute to Hitler during his visit to his *Heimatstadt* (hometown) Linz.

11. Document of resignation from Church membership

12. Rabka school with the banner which reads: Command of the Security police and Security Service in the General Government, School of the Security service, my father in the foreground shortly after his arrival (before the banner was installed).

13. The weapon the SS favoured was the Luger 08, cal 7.65

14. Top photograph shows the students in their classroom at Rabka. It is assumed that the man in the background (circled) is my father. It cannot be proved that the photograph below (shooting of a woman with her child) was taken at Rabka. The one below, shows a Nazi soldier setting his dogs on a Jewish prisoner at Rabka. The photograph at the bottom of the page shows the lesson, where members of the Einsatzgruppen were practising the shot-in-the neck technique on life victims. (This was not just 'taught' at Rabka but all over Europe)

15. Documents of two Jewish Kapos at Rabka, one of whom testified at my father's trial
16. Author 'at home', visiting Schloss Kremsegg in 2008
17. ODESSA's many faces, among them family members, Catholic Priest Alois Hudal, Millionaire-businessmen Hans Krupp von Bohlen, politician Eva Peron.
18. The killers of Rabka. Photographs of the deputies and main perpetrators of the Rabka killings
19. Documents proving my father's guilt
20. Photograph showing Jewish staff employed in the school (l to r) Lucia Goldfinger, Helena Baumann, and *Ada Rawicz* (nee Peller); *Lucia Goldfinger* and Ada Rawicz managed to escape and identify the murderers. The girl in the centre Helena Baumann, was murdered by SS at the school
21. Father celebrated his release from prison with a trip to the lakes, surrounded by his faithful supporters, among them my mother (circle)
22. The nightly vision, similar to the one I saw as a child
23. Father shortly before his death. He died of heart failure upon receiving new court summons in 1970 (background); the unmarked grave today
24. The company my father kept (see page 82)
25. Schloss Klaus became Heaven on earth for me
26. My friend Jack, friend of Dietrich Bonhoeffer, who helped me find freedom
27. Martin Luther and his infamous Anti-Semitic book '*Von den Juden und ihren Lügen'*; Austrian bishops welcoming Hitler to Austria
28. Map of small part of Upper Austria showing the environment I was born into

Picture credits[169]

Private collection: 1,3,4,6,8,9,12,13,15,16,18,19,20,22,23,24,25, 26, 28
Dr.Robin O'Neil: 7, 12
Mroczne sekrety willi "Tereska", Prezentacja multimedialna: 12,14, 19
www.freiburgs-geschichte.de: 27

[169] While every effort was made to trace the owners of copyrighted material, the author would like to apologise for any omissions and will be pleased to incorporate missing acknowledgments in any future editions

Appendix

Father's profile

Name	*Willhelm Oder*

18.3.1905	Born in Vöcklabruck, Upper Austria
27.7.1926	Marries Karoline (Lilly) Kump
11.9.1927	My first half-brother Wilhelm (Willi) was born
1928	Illegal membership of the NSDAP
4.2.1931	My second half-brother Peter was born
25.7.1934	Austrian Chancellor Engelbert Dollfuss assassinated by *The Illegals*. Wilhelm Oder arrested for conspiracy, sentenced to death.
12.3.1938	Anschluss of Austria & amnesty of all political prisoners saves Wilhelm from execution
18.03.1938	Joins SS on his birthday, aged 33
30.3.1938	Seconded to SS Sturm 52/5 St.Pölten
1.5.1938	Official NSDAP Membership. No. 6,271.713
1939	My half-brother Peter attends Adolf Hitler school. He and his brother Wilhelm join the Hitler Youth
1.7.1940	Seconded to 8th Totenkopf (SS) Division
3.11.1940	Completes training in Dachau
	Abandons his first wife Lilly and 2 children Wilhelm and Peter
July 1941	Transferred to Rabka, Poland
	Meets German secretary Käthe, who becomes pregnant
1.6.1942	Resigns membership of Catholic Church
5.11.1942	Becomes *Einsatzgruppenführer* of the SS School of murder
22.5.1943	Sends Käthe back to Germany for the birth of their love child Gesa
1943-1944	Transferred to Radom as KdS, commander of the SD
1945	Flees from Rabka, with other members of the

	Einsatzgruppen
9.4.1945	My eldest half brother Willy dies in a German trench at Niernburg an der Weser
5.5.1945	Claims to have been captured by Russians in Prague
1945	Escapes and flees to Hamburg, then goes into hiding in Austrian mountains
1946	Placed on the *Österreichische Fahndungsliste* (Austrian list of people wanted by the authorities (No. 80 on Wiesenthal's wanted list)
	Meets Karoline Pingitzer (Lilly number 2)
30.6.1947	Divorces his first wife Lilly No.1
4.3.1948	Arrested in Kremsmünster 1PM
19.10.1948	Extradition request by the Polish Government blocked by the *ODE* **SS** A
1948-1952	Imprisoned in the Hermann Goering Werke with Franz Stangl
4.2.1950	Asks Käthe to speak for him in court, then breaks off their relationship prior to marriage to Karoline Pingitzer, Lilly No 2
6.2.1951	Marriage application to Karoline
17.2.1951	Marries Karoline Pingitzer (my mother, now 8 months pregnant)
29.3.1951	Werner is born in Schloss Kremsegg, Upper Austria
2.7.1952	War crime trial in Linz. Found guilty of mistreatment of prisoners, but not guilty of murder
	Released on the same day at 7.30pm
1.5.1953	My sister Brigitte is born
1954	Has relationships with various women. Abandons Lilly No.2 and her children
1958	Divorced from Lilly No. 2
1959	Marries 'Elfi', wife No. 3
1970	Wiesenthal pushes for the reopening of trial due to concrete evidence of murder
1970	Upon receiving new court summons he dies of heart failure

Further reading

Aharoni Zvi, *Operation Eichmann,* Cassel & Co. London (1997)

Boremann Martin, *Leben gegen Schatten,* Paderborn Bonifatius GMBH, Verlag Paderborn (1996)

Buckingham Jamie, *A Way Through the Wilderness,* Kingsway Publication, Eastbourne, 1984

Mildred Cable & Frances French, *A Woman Who Laughed,* China Inland Mission, Religious tract Society, London (1934)

Eckman Ulf, *Beloved Hated Israel,* Ulf Eckman Ministries, Sweden (2004)

Elon Amon, *Herzl,* Holt Rhinehart & Whinston, Canada (1975)

Fraenkel Josef, *The Jews of Austria,* Vallentine, Mitchhell & Co, London (1967)

F.T.Grossmith, *The Cross and the Swastika,* H.E. Walter Limited, Worthing England (1984)

Küchler-Silbermann, Lena, *My hundred children,* Pan Books, London (1961)

Künstlich Chaim Benjamin, *L'CHAIM* © Chaim Benjamin Künstlich, Australia (2009)

Dr. Howard Morgan, *Lessons from the Olive tree,* Howard Morgan Ministries, Duluth, Georgia, USA (2001)

Dan Bar-On, *The Legacy of Silence,* Harvard University Press, New York (1989)

Pawson David, *Defending Christian Zionism,* Terra Nova Publishing, Bristol, England (2008)

Ray Juliana, *By Grace alone,*Ray Marshall Pickering, Basingstoke, England (1985)

Rapta Michal, Wojciech Tupta, Grzegorz Moskal, *Mroczne sekrety willi 'Tereska",* Rabka-Zdroj (2008)

Uki Goni, *The Real ODESSA,* Granta Books, London, (2002)

Wiesenthal Simon, *Doch die Mörder leben*, Herausgeber Josef Wechsberg, Droemerschen Verlagsanstalt TH. Mohndruck, Gütersloh, Germany (1967)

Wiesenthal Simon, *The Murderers Among us,* Pan Books Ltd, London, (1967)

Williamson Gordon*: Hitler's Instrument of terror,* Sidgwick & Jackson, London (1995)

Von Westhagen Dörte, *Die Kinder der Täter,* Deutscher Taschenburch Verlag, München (1987)

Dr. Robin O'Neil *Bełżec:* Steppingstone to Genocide

JewishGen © Robin O'Neil, Salisbury (2008)

-------- *Oscar Schindler: Steppingstone to Life* © Robin O'Neil, Salisbury (2010)

-------- *'Rabka Four.* A Warning from History, Spiderwize, UK, (2011)

Robin O'Neil, *The school of Murder*
www.jewishgen.org/yizkor/Galicia2/gal018.html.

Ron Rosenbaum, *Explaining Hitler: the search for the origins of his evil,* 1st edition, Random house, New York, (1998)

Dr. P. Rudolf Hundsdorfer O.S.B, *Das Stift unterm Hakenkreuz,* Stiftgymnasium Kremsmünster, Austria (2000)

For an extensive background to *Battling with Nazi Demons* read Robin O'Neil's book *The Rabka Four*, available from Spiderwize (enquiries@spiderwize.com) and all good book-stores.

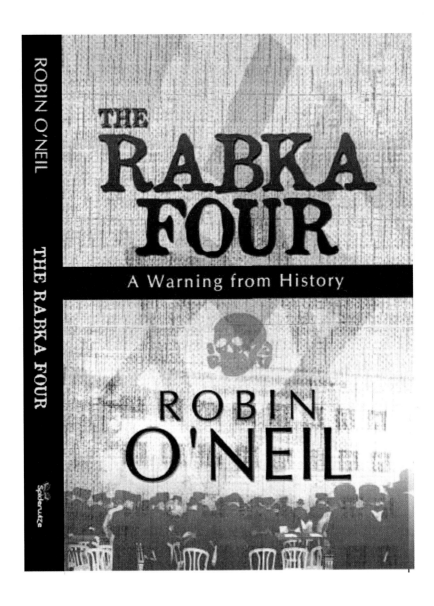